BIG
LIES

Mark Kurlansky has published 35 books,
including these titles for young readers:

Frozen in Time:
Clarence Birdseye's Outrageous Idea about Frozen Food

Battle Fatigue

World Without Fish

The Story of Salt

The Girl Who Swam to Euskadi

The Cod's Tale

Bugs in Danger:
Our Vanishing Bees, Butterflies, and Beetles

Tilbury House Publishers • Thomaston, Maine • Copyright © 2022 by Mark Kurlansky • Illustrations copyright © 2022 by Eric Zelz • All rights reserved. No part of this publication may be reproduced or transmitted in any form or by any means, electronic or mechanical, including photocopying, recording, or any information storage or retrieval system, without permission in writing from the publisher, except by a reviewer, who may quote brief passages in a review. • Library of Congress Control Number: 2022937862 • Interior design by Frame25 Productions; cover design by Notch Design • Printed in South Korea • First paperback printing August 2023 • 10 9 8 7 6 5 4 3 2 1

Photo Credits

Page 5, Henner Damke/Shutterstock • p.9, Vadim Nefedov/Alamy Stock Photo • p.16, Library of Congress, George Grantham Bain Collection • p.36, Glasshouse Images/Alamy Stock Photo • p.40, paseven/Shutterstock • p.58, Aunt Spray/Shutterstock • p.83, NASA/WMAP Science Team/Wikimedia Commons • p.127, Mikael Damkier/Shutterstock • p.135, Everett Collection/Shutterstock • p.138, Alamy Stock Photo • p.150, Alamy Stock Photo • p.155, Alpha Stock/Alamy Stock Photo • p.165, dpa Picture Alliance/Alamy Stock Photo • p.168, UPI/Alamy Stock Photo • p.169, Reuters/Alamy Stock Photo • p.172, NASA • p.176, Valery Brozhinsky/Shutterstock • p.183, Heritage Image Partnership Ltd/Alamy Stock Photo • p.199, CPA Media Pte Ltd/Alamy Stock Photo • p.204, Jeff Widener photo, The Associated Press • p.230, Robert Capa © International Center of Photography/Magnum Photos • p.231, Science and Society Picture Library • p.237, The Society for Co-operation in Russian and Soviet Studies/TopFoto • p.271, Aisyaquilumaranas/Shutterstock • p.274, Wikimedia Commons • p.280, 360b/Shutterstock • p.282, Keystone/Hulton Archive/Getty Images

BIG LIES

From Socrates to Social Media

MARK KURLANSKY

Illustrated by ERIC ZELZ

TILBURY HOUSE PUBLISHERS

REGINA: Why do people have to tell lies?

PETER: Usually because they want something
and are afraid the truth won't get it for them.

—from the 1963 movie *Charade*, written by Peter Stone,
starring Audrey Hepburn as Regina and Cary Grant as Peter

"Lies, my dear boy, are found out immediately, because
they are of two sorts. There are lies that have short
legs, and lies that have long noses. Your lie, as it
happens, is one of those that have a long nose."

—from *The Adventures of Pinocchio*, Carlo Collodi, 1883

Entreaty

"Truth tickles everyone's nostrils. The question is, how's it to be pulled from the heap?"

—Isaac Babel, "My First Goose"
(a story in *Red Cavalry*, 1926)

This book is full of ideas, facts, and opinions.

It would be easy just to read and believe it, but I ask you instead to consider as you read and to decide for yourself what to believe. Francis Bacon, a pioneer of the scientific method, wrote in 1612, "Read not to contradict and confute, nor to believe and take for granted, nor to find talk and discourse; but to weigh and consider."

That is how we struggle toward the truth, and it is that struggle that keeps the world from descending into chaos.

While it is often easy to spot a lie, it is harder to know what is true. Georg Wilhelm Friedrich Hegel, a still-admired nineteenth-century German philosopher, maintained that there is always an absolute truth, but it is not always possible to know it. That may be so, but the search for truth must be never-ending. We cannot achieve a well-ordered, healthy society for all the world's people if we do not keep asking what is true.

Often the question is why so many people choose to believe obvious lies. No lie becomes a big lie—a lie that undermines freedom, humanity, and the common good—without willing believers. Belief is a choice, and honesty begins in each of us. It is all too human to prefer an attractive lie to an inconvenient truth requiring difficult changes. When a lie provides comfort, consolation, excuses, or permission to do what you'd like to do anyway, who wouldn't prefer it? It is harder to question everything, but democracy depends on moral courage, independent thinking, and fair-mindedness. A lack of caring what is true or false is the undoing of democracy. Hannah Arendt, who fled Hitler's Germany and became one of the great philosophers of the twentieth century, wrote in *Origins of Totalitarianism,* "The ideal subject of totalitarianism is not the convinced Nazi, or the dedicated communist, but the people for whom the distinction between fact and fiction, true and false, no longer exists."

I hope that you will keep asking yourself **what is true as you** read this book and live your life.

—Mark Kurlansky

Contents

CHAPTER ONE

Masked Revelers in a CARNIVAL OF LIES

If you would be a real seeker after truth, it is necessary that at least once in your life you doubt, as far as possible, all things.

—René Descartes, *Principles of Philosophy*, 1644

Descartes was right. Question everything.

Perhaps that is more true today than ever. It seems that we are caught in a dance, spinning and leaping uncontrollably in an immense, unfathomable carnival of lies. Politicians lie, some rarely, some incessantly. There are lies to peddle bad medicines and lies that keep us away from good ones. Even the attribution to George Orwell of a famous epigram, "In a time of universal deceit—telling the truth is a revolutionary act," is a lie. The words are well suited for our times and sound like something Orwell might have said, but the quote cannot be found anywhere in his writing or his recorded utterances. In truth, it seems to have originated since his death in 1950—just another example of how skeptical we must be.

Nobel Prize–winning Yiddish novelist Isaac Bashevis Singer invented a character named Gimpel the Fool who believed everything he was told. When criticized for this, he said, "What do you mean! You want to call everyone a liar?" It would not be acceptable to call everyone a liar, but it is wise to question everything you are told.

In a traditional carnival, the revelers wear masks that conceal their true faces. This is also true in the carnival of lies. You cannot trust that the person whose opinions you are hearing or reading is who he or she pretends to be. We are told that we are being stalked by lizards, clowns, and space aliens or that an innocent pizza shop in Washington, DC may be the center of a dangerous conspiracy. Nothing should come as a surprise.

Lying is instinctive for humans. Child psychologist Jean Piaget concluded in 1932 that telling lies "is a natural tendency ... spontaneous and universal."

Children develop an ability to lie as they develop language and reasoning.

They lie so readily that they have to be taught and urged to tell the truth. It is the rare child who is so instinctively truthful that he or she must be taught to lie.

Humans are not the only deceptive animals. Deception arrived to us through evolution. Foxes, ravens, and crows are famous for deceptive practices. Have you ever seen a dog bark and growl and bare its teeth simply because it is frightened? Animals from insects to mammals sometimes pretend ferocity to scare off enemies. They are bluffing. Other animals pretend to be less aggressive than they are, and a number of species pretend to be dead when threatened.

Some animals are camouflaged from birth to blend into their habitats, but others can manipulate their appearance to match conditions. Chameleons, of which there are 202 known species, change their appearance in reaction to temperature or social signaling, or as a sign of aggression or submission, or sometimes just to blend into a background—but also to deceive other animals. The octopus, without shell or skeleton, relies on deceit to survive, adopting various shapes and colors to fool predators and prey.

Some deceptions are thoughtlessly inherited. In what is called Batesian mimicry, for example, a harmless butterfly emerges from its cocoon with the markings of a poisonous one to scare off aggressors.

Unconscious deception evolved into conscious lying with the development of the neocortex in the higher primates.

Some monkeys will shriek out alarm cries to make their comrades run for safety when there is no danger but only food the monkey doesn't want to share. But we humans are the most highly evolved liars.

Evolution, as defined by nineteenth-century British biologist Charles Darwin, operates through natural selection. Any genetic modification that increases an individual's chances of surviving and reproducing is likely to be passed on to subsequent generations. In similar fashion, the ability to deceive has been passed down through endless generations of human beings because it is a successful strategy. We have evolved into liars because a creature that lies has a better chance of surviving than a wholly honest one. Human beings are much better at lying than all other species because of our advanced communication skills, starting with our ability to speak.

An octopus deceives with color changes. Human deception is more complicated.

Bluffing, exaggerating, bragging, and out-and-out lying are common tools for competing. We sometimes even lie to ourselves. Psychiatrist Arnold Ludwig wrote, "Fantasy often represents a convenient way for man to temporarily lie to himself in order to make life more palatable. Our innate love of storytelling shows how drawn to lying we are." Everyone lies one way or another—falsifies a number, exaggerates to make a point, doctors the truth to make it less incriminating or embarrassing, or lies by omission, deliberately neglecting to mention inconvenient or unfavorable truths. The person who never lies would be unbearable. We tell people they are looking well even when they aren't, because we think they need to hear it. We say a ghastly dinner was delicious, an ugly home charming, a boring visit lovely.

> # When the truth is harsh, a lie often seems preferable.
> ## That is the human flaw that gives a liar the needed opening.

While the acceptance of a "little white lie" is generally pragmatic, even polite, it conditions us to accept more consequential lies that might sound preferable to the truth—for example, that there is no climate change, or that climate change isn't caused by humans, or that there's nothing to be done about it so let's not even try.

The Old Testament denounces all lying, but the fifth-century Talmud, the other underpinning of Jewish law, cites instances when lying is permissible—for example, to avoid appearing boastful. If asked about intimate relations with your spouse, the Talmud maintains that you are not obligated to tell the truth. Lying is also permissible, the Talmud maintains, in the service of peacemaking.

Thomas Aquinas, a thirteenth-century theologian considered one of the greatest Christian thinkers, believed that lies are permissible when told to be helpful or as a joke. Only when the intent is malicious did he consider lying a mortal sin. But Immanuel Kant, an eighteenth-century German philosopher and great moralist, distinguished himself by insisting that lying is always wrong. He was not interested in distinctions between harmless and harmful lies, insisting that all lies are harmful, "for a lie always harms another, if not some other particular man, still it harms mankind generally,

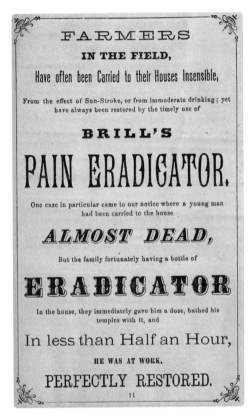

Advertising has always occupied the gray area between exaggeration and outright lying—or sometimes, as in this nineteenth-century ad for Brill's Pain Eradicator, not so gray.

for it vitiates the source of law itself." In other words, since laws are based on truth, any violation of truth undermines the premise of a legal society. Kant also said that any lie undermines the dignity of others.

Numerous professions thrive on lying. Advertisers make false claims or just exaggerated ones. Imagine trying to convince someone to buy a car because it gets fairly good gas mileage, is as comfortable as the next car, and sells for a price typical of cars of its class. This may be an accurate description of most cars, but it doesn't make a customer want to buy that model.

> Virtually all politicians lie to a greater or lesser degree. Dictators lie to construct a false reality that justifies their dictatorship, but sometimes a dictator can **tell a truth** that an elected official would not dare to tell.

In 1992, when the Soviet Union, which had subsidized Cuba, was in the final stages of collapse, Cuban dictator Fidel Castro could have claimed that the Soviet empire could still survive, or that Russian money would flow to Cuba anyway, or that Cuba would be fine without it, but he didn't. Instead, he said in a speech that Cuba was entering "a special period in time of peace." He said there would be a lack of oil, that cars would not run, that there would be food shortages, that people would be hungry and times would be hard. It all came to pass as predicted, but Castro's support remained strong because he had told the truth.

Fidel Castro was popular despite the slums in Havana and tough times in Cuba.

This goes against the long-standing playbook of political leadership, but it worked in that instance. In truth, it worked partly because Castro was a dictator—though this does not detract from Castro's originality, because most dictators prefer to lie. Joseph Stalin, who ruled the Soviet Union from 1927 until 1953, spent that quarter century lying to the Russian people about the dire state of their economy. But Castro's truth strategy would probably not have worked well in a democracy, the leader of which faces constant challenges. Other politicians would have come forward with lies about how much better life would be under their leadership, and since that is what people prefer to hear, the truthful politician would last only until the next election.

This was clearly the politics of former US president Donald Trump, who, according to *The Washington Post* Fact Checker Team, made 30,573 false or misleading claims in his four years in office, including 503 on the day before the November 2020 reelection vote. He told people that drastic adjustments to address climate change were unnecessary because climate change was a hoax. He either knew that climate change is real or didn't know and didn't care. Calling it a hoax was a tactic, just like his insistence that the coronavirus pandemic was exaggerated. With him as America's leader, there was no need to make inconvenient changes to lifestyles and livelihoods. And isn't that what people would prefer to hear if they can somehow convince themselves it is true?

Sooner or later the truth may become inescapable, but a practiced deceiver lies for today, not tomorrow, knowing that the deceived will be no more eager than the deceiver to acknowledge that they've been duped.

Give them another lie tomorrow with which to avoid the truth, and they may take it. In the meantime, reap the rewards today.

In 1513 Niccolò Machiavelli, an Italian Renaissance diplomat, published *The Prince*, a cynical and highly influential guide to statecraft that advised deception and ruthlessness. It is still read today, and many political leaders have been influenced by it to a much greater degree than they care to admit. Machiavelli advised the ruler to "be a great pretender and dissembler; and men are so simple and so obedient to present necessities that he who deceives will always find someone who will let himself be deceived." From the Medici rulers of Machiavelli's Florence to modern demagogues around the world, this approach has proven successful. If a lie is appealing, followers will be

The title page of a 1550 edition of *The Prince*. Five hundred years after its initial publication, it remains a go-to playbook for autocrats.

found. As Machiavelli put it, "the deceiver will always find someone ready to be deceived."

There are two main categories of lies, personal and public. The former are lies we tell friends, family, teachers, bosses, neighbors. We're all familiar with them. But this book is about public lies—lies told by governments, political movements, members of the media, other influential public figures, and corporations. These are lies told to avoid responsibility, to win elections, to disguise true intent, to distract the public from things the liar wants to hide, to change our perceptions of truth, to create chaos and confusion, to gain and retain power and wealth. Public lies— big lies—threaten democracy and ideals of liberty and justice. They have a very long history, but they have never been more prolific than today.

Much of social media is between individuals, which is how social media was intended to be used. There is bragging, lying, and a lot of lying by omission (things that are deliberately not said). There is the party she said she went to but didn't, the faked athletic achievement, the fifty-pound fish that really wasn't caught, the firing from a job that a LinkedIn profile fails to mention. These are personal lies, which come with many shades and distinctions. Is a lie justified when the deceived person has no right to know the truth? Are you required to tell the bully how much money is in your pocket? The ethics of personal lying are nuanced, but personal lies are not what I want to write about.

What concerns this book is lying by governments, public leaders, and private organizations with **political agendas** distorting the news or science or public events. That is the real danger, the **public danger.** This book is about that kind of lying, which can destabilize the world.

Until recently, private lying was for private communications and public lying was for public platforms. Books, pamphlets, and television were for public communications, not private lies. Radio was always a little different. Public information could be broadcast under the guise of an informal conversation. That was why President Franklin Roosevelt in the 1930s called his political messages on radio "chats." Radio hosts can slip by the most outrageous public lies in a casual manner, as though what they're saying is common knowledge, something everyone should know.

A gathering of Socialists in Union Square, New York City, May 1912. Whether the speaker's platform is a streetcorner or Facebook, democracy depends on listeners who care what is fact or fiction, true or false.

Social media platforms have taken this further. Designed for private communications, they can broadcast public statements to millions in the form of a casual comment. They can be used to tell public lies in the guise of private ones. Twitter, like most social media platforms, is designed to sound private and chatty. It is full of private lies and private truths—personal conversations. But it can be used for public lies, often told in a vernacular that does not sound like an official statement.

Public liars
have always looked for
casual ways
to slip lies into public discourse, and it has
never been easier than
social media
makes it today.

The history of political lying reveals two reliable principles. The first is that the bigger the lie, the more followers it will attract. Only a few are interested in a slight deception, but if a truly outrageous claim is made, it will find many believers. According to Adolf Hitler, who coined the term "big lie" in the 1925 outline of his political program *Mein Kampf*, an outrageous lie succeeds because no one can believe its perpetrator "could have the impudence to distort the truth so infamously."

WHILE ROME BURNED

To this day it is said that the Emperor Nero let Rome burn. It has even been said that he played the fiddle (which had not yet been invented) or the harp while the great city burned. The fire in AD 64 started in the Circus Maximus, a huge racetrack for charioteers, and spread quickly to the shops and apartment blocks nestled under the circus walls. Hundreds were killed, and hundreds of thousands of Rome's more than one million residents were left homeless.

The story that Nero started the fire came centuries later, probably from a Christian source. There is no evidence of his guilt; in fact, Nero was in the nearby town of Antium at the time, though of course he could have told a lackey to start the fire while he was gone. What Nero did do was lie. He falsely claimed that Christians had set the fire, and he used this as an excuse to arrest, torture, and execute hundreds of them because he believed they had become too powerful. There is no evidence that Christians had anything to do with the fire.

The second principle is that the more often a lie is repeated, the greater the number of people who will believe it. Catherine de' Medici, of the ruling sixteenth-century Florentine family, was a generation younger than Machiavelli but clearly familiar with his work. She became the queen of France and is quoted as saying, "A false report, if believed during three days, may be a great service to a government." A lie repeated regularly in a short period of time begins to sound like a truth. Many others have made similar observations about the power of repeated lies. Ironically, Catherine may never have made this often-cited observation; it may be one of the many things falsely attributed to this famous queen. (It is often said that she introduced Italian food to France, but since she arrived with an entourage of only French chefs, this too is probably untrue.)

But it *is* true that the more often a lie is repeated, the more likely it is to be accepted as true. That is the power of the internet. Think of the power of repeating a lie a hundred million times in a few days via social media.

The story of their involvement was a useful lie, one that was echoed in 1933 when, after gaining power in Germany, Adolf Hitler used the burning of the Reichstag, the German parliament building, as an excuse to suspend constitutional rights because of a communist attack. Hitler's accusation of the communists was almost certainly a lie, but did Hitler's Nazis actually start the fire or merely take advantage of it? Whatever the truth may be, the phrase "Reichstag fire" has come to signify a false-flag operation, an "inside job" concocted by an authoritarian government as an excuse to persecute opponents.

Of course, public figures have always found ways to spread lies, and some of those lies have been accepted as history. The Americas are named after Amerigo Vespucci, who was supposed to have been the first European to make landfall in South America, arriving in 1497, one year before Christopher Columbus. The source of this claim was Vespucci himself, in a 1504 letter that historians now believe to have been a lie. He did go to South America, but later than Columbus.

Lying comes naturally to humans, and we are uniquely skilled liars, but we are also uniquely skilled at seeing through lies. While the internet is a great tool for lying, it is a valuable tool for exposing lies as well.

FOUNDING FIBS

It is common to teach American schoolchildren not to lie by telling them a lie. The lie is that George Washington chopped down a cherry tree as a boy; when his father confronted him, young George is supposed to have said "I cannot tell a lie" and confessed to the deed, whereupon his father said that his son's honesty was worth a thousand cherry trees. None of this happened.

The story was invented by Mason Locke Weems, who published *The Life and Memorable Actions of George Washington* in 1800, a year after Washington's death. The cherry tree anecdote did not appear until the fifth edition of the book in 1806. The book sold spectacularly well and was read by generation after generation of schoolchildren.

The book included other fictitious stories, such as a tale of the general kneeling in prayer at Valley Forge with a Quaker who was so moved that he gave up pacifism. Weems may have been reaching for what Plato, in his 375 BCE dialogue with Socrates, *The Republic*, called a grand lie. Plato quoted Socrates as saying, "We want one single grand lie which will be believed by everybody." To Plato, a grand or noble lie is one that gives national or civic identity.

Plato's suggestion was that a nation needs a few myths, even if untrue, to build an identity. In *The Republic,* Plato argued that it is the duty of the state to cultivate nobility, and people too backward to appreciate this must be lied to. This argument has had the probably unforeseen consequence throughout history of lies being fed to the masses. The lies might or might not be noble by Plato's definition, but they are always lies.

In 1800 it was strongly believed that America, this new country, needed some myths and mythic heroes. Washington—tall, elegant, finely dressed, well-spoken, and at the center of history—always attracted lies. He did have ivory dentures but, contrary to common belief, never wore wooden teeth, which would not have worked well. He could not possibly have spent a night in all the bedrooms that boasted "George Washington slept here." Fortunes were made in the nineteenth century with fake portraits for which Washington allegedly posed.

Washington was a target for liars even before his ultimate victory over the British forces in the Revolutionary War. In one story he fainted with fear at the appearance of a British general. In 1776 an obvious forgery appeared, called *Letters from General Washington to Several of His Friends in the Year 1776*. According to the completely fabricated story, Washington fled at the first sign of General Cornwallis, leaving behind his manservant, Billy Lee, and his possessions. It was Lee who revealed among the possessions a packet of letters from Washington.

The letters showed him to be a coward and a British sympathizer. "Tell me," he wrote in a letter to a farm manager, "Am I, do you think, more subject to fear than other men? For I will not conceal it from you, that at this moment I feel myself a very coward."

The letters showed that he considered the war lost and only continued by feeding lies to his supporters. He searched for a way to resign his commission. He revealed to his wife, Martha, that he longed to make peace with his British friends. He seemed to worship King George III. "I love my King. You know I do: a soldier, a good man cannot but love him."

Published in England, the letters were dismissed as forgeries by the British press but sold well in America. Washington laughed them off, but they reemerged in 1795, during his second term as president, in the middle of a scorching political fight over a treaty to normalize relations with Britain. Alexander Hamilton was physically attacked, and mobs burned the British flag in the street. Washington tried to remain neutral, but angry opponents, believing he supported the treaty, reprinted the 1776 forgeries to prove that he had always been a pro-British hypocrite. Washington again dismissed the letters, seemingly unable to believe that such lies could endure, but they plagued the last two years of his presidency. He finally denounced the fraud on his last day in office, then spent the rest of his life believing the forged letters had damaged his reputation.

FROM **RUSSIA** WITH **LOVE**

PART 1: THE CAMERA ZOOMS IN ON A LARGE DARK BUILDING **SOMEWHERE IN MOSCOW.** ON THE IMPOSING FRONT DOOR IS AN **INSIGNIA OF A SWORD AND SHIELD—** "THE PARTY'S SWORD AND SHIELD," AS VLADIMIR LENIN CALLED IT LONG AGO.

LENIN AND THE PARTY ARE LONG GONE, BUT THE **SWORD AND SHIELD SURVIVED** . . .

IN SOVIET UNION TIMES IT WAS THE **SYMBOL OF THE KGB AND THE FSB**, BUT IT HAS NOW BECOME THE EMBLEM FOR VLADIMIR PUTIN'S **SECRET POLICE**.

THE CAMERA ENTERS THE BUILDING, *FLOATS UP TWO FLIGHTS OF STAIRS*, AND EXITS THE STAIRWELL ONTO THE *THIRD FLOOR*.

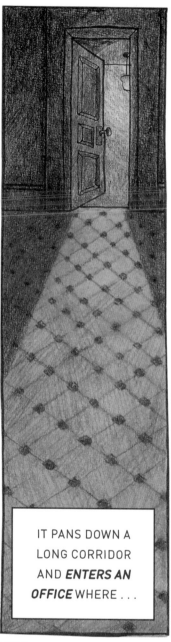

IT PANS DOWN A
LONG CORRIDOR
AND ***ENTERS AN
OFFICE*** WHERE . . .

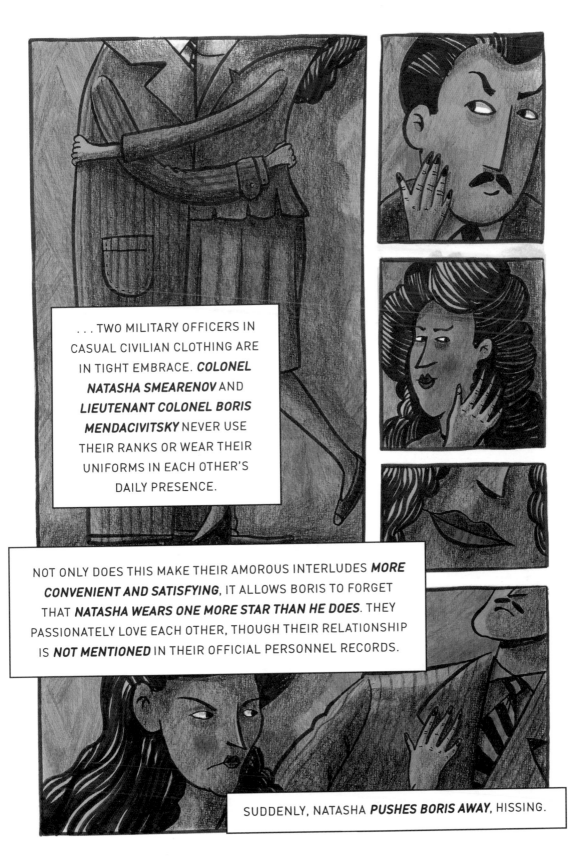

... TWO MILITARY OFFICERS IN CASUAL CIVILIAN CLOTHING ARE IN TIGHT EMBRACE. *COLONEL NATASHA SMEARENOV* AND *LIEUTENANT COLONEL BORIS MENDACIVITSKY* NEVER USE THEIR RANKS OR WEAR THEIR UNIFORMS IN EACH OTHER'S DAILY PRESENCE.

NOT ONLY DOES THIS MAKE THEIR AMOROUS INTERLUDES *MORE CONVENIENT AND SATISFYING*, IT ALLOWS BORIS TO FORGET THAT *NATASHA WEARS ONE MORE STAR THAN HE DOES*. THEY PASSIONATELY LOVE EACH OTHER, THOUGH THEIR RELATIONSHIP IS *NOT MENTIONED* IN THEIR OFFICIAL PERSONNEL RECORDS.

SUDDENLY, NATASHA *PUSHES BORIS AWAY*, HISSING.

THE MAJOR **STARES AT THEM** FOR EMPHASIS, THEN LEAVES.

NATASHA AND BORIS WAIT UNTIL HIS **FOOTFALLS RECEDE**, THEN **RETURN TO THEIR EMBRACE**.

TO BE CONTINUED . . .

CHAPTER TWO

The ENLIGHTENMENT and the UNENLIGHTENED

*Ignorance more frequently begets
confidence than does knowledge.*
—Charles Darwin, *The Descent of Man*, 1871

The explosion of social media seems to have ushered us into a new age of lying.

It has certainly become faster and easier to spread lies. Surprisingly, though, most of the lies themselves aren't new. They tend to be old-fashioned and unoriginal. The polarized divide that right-wing politicians are exploiting in the twenty-first century dates back three hundred years.

A shift in thinking known as the Enlightenment took root in the seventeenth century and has endured to this day. The Enlightenment promoted individualism, egalitarianism, and reason. The American and French revolutions were both informed and partly caused by the Enlightenment.

When Thomas Jefferson wrote in the US Declaration of Independence that "all men are created equal" and that they have "inalienable rights," **he was expressing enlightenment ideals.**

Conservatives, monarchists, and most state-supported religions denounced the declaration.

The US constitution is also a product of the Enlightenment. The concept of secularism, the separation of church and state—that is, that the state has no right to impose a religion on its citizens—is a product of the Enlightenment. The idea that science is a way to reveal truths and that it, rather than religion, explains natural phenomena and the universe is at the heart of the Enlightenment.

Leading philosophers and mathematicians such as René Descartes (1596–1650), Thomas Hobbes (1588–1679), John Locke (1632–1704), Jean-Jacques Rousseau (1712–1778), and Immanuel Kant (1724–1804) helped define and lead the Enlightenment. So did scientists such as Francis Bacon (1561–1626), one of the first, perhaps *the* first, to say that truth is not a matter of belief but is found by testing verifiable phenomena. He died in such an experiment, stopping his coach in the snow outside London because he was suddenly seized by the idea that cold could preserve food. The chicken he packed with snow was preserved, but he wasn't. He died of pneumonia after his experiment.

Other giants of modern science include Isaac Newton (1643–1727), the founder of physics; Robert Boyle (1627–1691), the founder of modern chemistry; Antonie van Leeuwenhoek (1632–1723), microscope builder and founder of microbiology; Carolus Linnaeus (1707–1778), founder of the taxonomic system for naming and classifying organisms that we still

use; Humphry Davy (1778–1829), the discoverer of key elements in the periodic table; and Charles Darwin (1809–1882), the founder of modern biology. They were all products of the Enlightenment.

The world we live in—its politics, science, the ideals to which we aspire, the things we learn in school—comes from the Enlightenment.

We still believe in the Enlightenment, **though we seldom feel the need to say so.** What is more surprising is that opposition to the Enlightenment **has also survived.**

There has always been a divide between pro- and anti-Enlightenment thinking. The overwhelming majority of people, if asked, will say they believe in science, democracy, equal rights, social justice, and the removal of religion from government—all the ideals of the US constitution—but a vociferous and determined minority oppose these cherished beliefs. Not only do they speak out against those beliefs, they denounce the Enlightenment by name, in social-media posts and elsewhere.

The only major country with an openly anti-Enlightenment government was Tsarist Russia, though anti-Enlightenment politicians appeared here and there in other countries. The Romanov dynasty, which ruled Russia from 1613 until its overthrow in the 1917 revolution, was staunchly anti-Enlightenment. A Russian could be arrested and imprisoned for reading such Enlightenment writers as Rousseau, Hobbes, and Johann Wolfgang von Goethe (1749–1832), the most esteemed German writer and a pioneering scientist.

The opponents of Enlightenment, from Russian tsars to demagogues today, have been privileged authoritarians who have tried to rally to their cause people who belong to no labor union, political party, or social group; people who are not financially successful or even comfortable; people who feel that no one speaks for them.

People left behind by the Enlightenment are easy to convince that its basic premise must be wrong

and somehow biased against them.
Ironically, the people seeking to convince them are often wealthy and successful.

For two centuries such opportunists have fed the alienation of the underprivileged and disaffected with tales of conspiracy, fabricating one lie after another about plots against them. Adolf Hitler advised that propaganda should be aimed at the least educated and least intelligent. In *Mein Kampf* he wrote, "All propaganda should be popular and should adapt its intellectual level to the receptive ability of the least intellectual of those whom it is desired to address."

If, when you listen to a demagogue, you think that what he or she is saying makes no sense, you should understand that he or she is not speaking to you. When well-educated people support a demagogue's lies and distortions, you can be certain that their reasons for doing so are cynical. Most politicians who support an extremist party leader probably do not believe the things he or she says. They may be afraid of incurring the wrath of their political base or their big donors. They may also be opportunistic, believing their public agreement will earn them votes or other advantages. They may think the demagogue's front-page harangues will distract the media from things they'd rather not talk about or have to defend. The demagogue himself may not believe most of what he says or may be too incurious to care—or maybe his only belief is in what works to his advantage today.

DEMONETIZATION

As most any con artist knows, the poor and uneducated who feel misery in their lives are the most likely purchasers of a bottle of snake oil. They are not looking for truth; they are looking for miracles, someone to come along and change the world. This is where demagogues find supporters, as is seen all over the world.

In 2016, Indian Prime Minister Narendra Modi announced a policy known as demonetization. Under this policy, as of November 8, 2016, all 500- and 1,000-rupee banknotes of the Mahatma Gandhi Series would no longer be legal tender. Holders of these currency notes would have until the end of the year to exchange them for newly designed 500- and 2,000-rupee notes at a bank. Many of the most impoverished Indians had no bank account and had to find someone to exchange their discontinued currency, which led to many hours of standing in lines. For the business class and affluent Indians, it was simply a bank transaction.

Adolf Hitler in Berlin, May 1, 1934. Hitler could not have started a world war and caused the deaths of millions without popular support.

The Enlightenment removed the aristocracy from power, so aristocrats and admirers of aristocracy opposed it. The Loyalists who opposed the American Revolution and the Royalists who supported French royalty, opposed the French Revolution, and plagued French politics throughout the nineteenth century were rejecting the Enlightenment. When a politician insists that democracy is unfair and doesn't work, he or she is rejecting the Enlightenment. He or she is following a long line of anti-Enlightenment leaders who have tried to cast doubts about voting in order to undermine the idea of democracy.

The Enlightenment weakened religious authority by asserting that science—provable and testable knowledge, not the conjectures of religion—holds the key to unlock the truths of our universe.

They did not pay for much with cash anyway. But for impoverished farmers with small harvests of cash crops such as cotton, this was a disaster. They lived in a cash world.

Here is the strange part. The moneyed classes, who had never felt good about Modi, did not like demonetization and claimed it would wreak havoc on the economy, which it did. But the policy was supported by the poor. Why? Because Modi presented himself as being on their side and against the moneyed establishment. He told them this was a war against "black money"—the corrupt gains of the wealthy. He said he would take this black money away from the rich and distribute it among the poor. Poor farmers, whose circumstances are so desperate that more than a million have committed suicide by swallowing pesticides or hanging themselves, cheered demonetization, which was making their lives even harder; and even though no black money ever turned up for them in any form, they went on cheering this policy that they believed was standing up to the rich on their behalf. Modi was "the strong leader" who would stand up to the dangers from the Muslim minority (another invention of his) and would stand up to Pakistan. Now he would also stand up to the black money. He won reelection in 2019 by a record landslide.

Science deniers—whether they reject Darwin and evolution or the fact that carbon emissions are wreaking havoc on the climate or the proven effectiveness of a vaccine—are rejecting the Enlightenment.

The fabricated claim that an elite group called the Illuminati conspired to establish the Enlightenment through trickery has been around for almost 250 years. The idea may never have been more popular than today. An Illuminati Facebook page has garnered more than 3.4 million likes, and the Illuminati conspiracy is extremely popular on YouTube.

There really was a secret society called the Bavarian Illuminati. We still do not know who its members were. Goethe was thought to have been one, although there is no proof of this. The purpose of the Illuminati was to promote the Enlightenment, but fear and denunciation of the society long outlasted the society itself, which existed only from 1776 to 1785. The founder, Adam Weishaupt, was a German law professor who strongly believed in the ideas of the Enlightenment. The society's membership may have reached 2,500 at its height but was just a few hundred through most of its existence. Karl Theodor, Duke of Bavaria, banned secret societies in 1785, and the Illuminati were suppressed and destroyed.

But no sooner were they destroyed than conspiracists began to insist that they still operated in secret and were hugely powerful. They were said to be the authors of the French Revolution. Based on absolutely nothing other than his Enlightenment thinking, Thomas Jefferson was accused of belonging to the Illuminati. In 1798 a Boston minister, Jedidiah Morse, warned that the new country of America needed to rally and defend itself against the Illuminati, an odd position considering that America itself was a product of the Enlightenment.

The Illuminati were said to have infiltrated other secretive groups such as the Freemasons. Freemasons have been under suspicion by the same people who decry the Illuminati, and for some of the same reasons.

Freemason conspiracy theory symbology.

They appear to support the ideals of the Enlightenment, their membership and practices are secret, and they have secret signs and symbols. They were founded in the eleventh century by bricklayers who did not belong to any of the workers' guilds and who traveled from place to place looking for work, eventually organizing into "lodges" in various locations. At first, they were literally free masons, non-union bricklayers, but their purposes, membership, and agenda greatly expanded with time. They appeared to have no national allegiance and so were labeled "rootless," a slur also frequently hurled at Jews. Their membership was secular and open to a variety of religions including Judaism, so they were constantly attacked by Christian churches. Freethinkers such as Voltaire

(1694–1778), who had an important impact on the French Revolution, were Masons. Masons also played a role in the American Revolution. Paul Revere, Ethan Allen, Roger Sherman, Benjamin Franklin, Patrick Henry, and George Washington were all Revolutionary leaders who were Freemasons. The Marquis de Lafayette and Alexander Hamilton may also have been Freemasons. The mysterious pyramid with an eye on the top, featured on the dollar bill, is thought to be a Freemason symbol. At least, there is no other explanation for it.

The anti-Freemason cause grew so strong in America that an Anti-Masonic Party was founded in 1826 and held, in 1831, the first national nominating convention of any US political party. But in 1832, running almost entirely on opposition to Freemasons, the party won only seven electoral votes, all from the state of Vermont, and it faded soon after.

One of the many lies levied against the Freemasons was that they were controlled by the Illuminati. Unlike the Freemasons, however, the Illuminati no longer existed.

These conspiracy theories may sound like something from the past, but periodically they reemerge.

In the 1950s, under the influence of a Canadian conspiracy theorist named William Guy Carr, the American Christian right warned of the danger from Freemasons, Illuminati, and Jews behind an "international Communist conspiracy." Although the threat of Communism has diminished, theorists continue to warn of "a new world order" engineered by Masons, Illuminati, and Jews.

⟡⟡⟡⟡⟡⟡⟡⟡⟡⟡⟡⟡⟡⟡⟡⟡⟡⟡⟡⟡⟡⟡⟡⟡⟡⟡⟡⟡⟡⟡⟡⟡⟡⟡⟡⟡⟡

SEND IN THE CLOWNS

You may not see anything wrong with clowns, but some people do. They do not have human faces. They smile for no obvious reason, as though there is a joke only they know. And they often have weird hair.

In August 2016, a clown named Gags stood on a street corner in Green Bay, Wisconsin. Gags was an intentionally creepy promotion for a low-budget horror film, and he must have been successful, because the Green Bay police department was flooded with 911 calls, although he did nothing more than hand out balloons.

Complaints of his menacing ways spread via social media, and a nation-wide clown panic ensued. Fear of clowns is so well established that there is even a word for it—coulrophobia (from the Greek words *kōlobatheron*, stilts, and *phobia*, fear). With social media help, this longtime fear of clowns surged.

Later that same month, numerous children in Greenville, South Carolina, reported sighting a group of clowns "whispering" and "making strange noises." The police investigated but could find no clowns. This did not stop many panicked locals from concluding that evil clowns were luring children into the woods. In Macon, Georgia, there was a report of clowns threatening children at a bus stop. Anonymous tips of clown sightings spread panic throughout the Carolinas and across the country, although no children were missing.

Social-media posts propelled the chaos, but it is difficult to say how many of the reports were sincere and how many were mischievous or malicious. Clearly there were some of each. A man in Winston-Salem was arrested for making a false police report.

The next month a woman spotted a clown by the back gate of her apartment complex in Gainesville, Florida, while taking out the trash. "He had on all black—he had a black-and-white mask on with clown hair, and he was just staring at us, making noises, trying to get our attention." She called 911, but police could find no clown. Soon after, a video was posted on Facebook that showed someone in a clown mask standing by trees at night, and this immediately got 1.2 million hits. Media tended to report these clown sightings with no attempt to verify them. Child-menacing clowns were reported in Georgia, Arkansas, Mississippi, Missouri, Louisiana, Texas, Virginia, West Virginia, Maryland, Delaware, New Jersey, Massachusetts, Rhode Island, New York, Pennsylvania, Ohio, Indiana, Michigan, Minnesota, Illinois, Iowa, Nebraska, Kansas, Colorado, Utah, Idaho, and Oregon.

Some communities banned the wearing of clown costumes. More clown threats appeared on social media. One Facebook group, with members claiming to be clowns, threatened to kill teachers and kidnap children, but it never happened.

Some jokesters have been arrested for dressing as clowns to frighten people, but no one has found any evidence of a conspiracy of evil clowns. There have been numerous robberies in which the perpetrators wore clown masks, though this is not a new phenomenon. And there were earlier clown panics, even before the age of social media. One in the 1980s was caused by a rumor that clowns were kidnapping children for "satanic rituals," but no such activity was ever uncovered. No evidence has ever been found of evil clowns attacking children.

Fear of the Illuminati may seem old fashioned next to fear of the deep state, but the fear still exists. In the 1970s, *The Illuminatus Trilogy,* by Robert Shea and Robert Anton Wilson—a work of fiction rooted in a smattering of facts, including the identification of Adam Weishaupt as the society's founder—revived paranoia about the Illuminati. Some of Dan Brown's bestselling novels and film adaptations are about a fictional modern Illuminati plot against the Catholic Church. Although he is enlarging on lies promoted by far-right conspiracists with a blatant political agenda, Brown's own agenda appears to be more commercial—people enjoy conspiracies, and they sell well. Most people—including most of Brown's fans—probably do not take the Illuminati conspiracy seriously. As with all little lies, though, the conspiracy theory serves a larger, more malevolent purpose. It helps to spread the false impression that the Enlightenment, rather than representing society's deeply held values, is a conspiracy promoted by an elite few.

Today's far-right conspiracy fabricators are more likely to smear pop-culture celebrities than Goethe and Jefferson. They like villains the public can relate to, people seen on YouTube and television. Jay Z, Beyoncé, and Kanye West are all said to be Illuminati. They deny it, but then, they would, wouldn't they?

Recently hoaxers revealed that the US government was cancelled in the 1860s, and the country has been run by the Illuminati ever since. Few people really believe in the Illuminati; it is more of an amusement than anything else. But it is one more little lie to underpin bigger, more malicious lies.

BY ANY OTHER NAME

One way to make an old trick new is to give it a new name. Right-wing American politicians have identified a replacement for the Illuminati called the deep state. This new imagined adversary, a secret cabal of unelected technocrats and bureaucrats who pull the strings of government, must be confronted at every turn in the name of freedom.

The term "deep state" was first heard in Turkey, where, after World War I and the collapse of the Ottoman Empire, a more progressive republic was established under Mustafa Ataturk. A right-wing group opposing democracy organized in the 1950s and called themselves *derin devlet*, Turkish for deep state. The group—largely military people who fomented riots and violent unrest—concentrated their attacks on government officials who they claimed were communists. Derin devlet extremists were blamed for thousands of deaths.

In the 1970s, Russian defectors started claiming that the KGB was a deep state controlling the Soviet government. Interestingly, after the Soviet Union fell, Russia eventually slipped into the hands of a key former KGB agent, Vladimir Putin.

The term did not appear in the US until 2014, toward the end of the Obama presidency. That was when former Republican congressional aide Mike Lofgren, who retired in 2011 and became an outspoken critic of the Republican Party, wrote an essay titled "Anatomy of the Deep State." Lofgren described a different kind of deep state, one comprised of wealthy financial and industrial leaders who manipulated government openly.

The deep state, wrote Lofgren, is not "a secret, conspiratorial cabal; the state within a state is hiding mostly in plain sight, and its operators mainly act in the light of day. It is not a tight-knit group and has no clear objective. Rather, it is a sprawling network, stretching across the government and into the private sector." To Lofgren the enemy was on Wall Street and in Silicon Valley. This was not a new concept; it was similar to the warning sounded by President Dwight Eisenhower in his 1961 farewell address, in which he cautioned future presidents to "guard against the acquisition of unwarranted influence, whether sought or unsought, by the military-industrial complex."

But "deep state" was redefined yet again by Donald Trump and his supporters, this time as a secret organization of the wealthy and powerful that was plotting against him. This deep state, we were told, had long been active and was responsible for many of the worst decisions of the US government. The deep state had urged the war in Vietnam, was behind Al Qaeda and the 9/11 attacks, duped the George W. Bush administration into believing the lie of Saddam Hussein's weapons of mass destruction, and tricked President Obama into widening the drone war in the Middle East. The FBI investigation of the Trump campaign's connections to Russia was a deep-state plot to take down Trump. The goals of the deep state are to promote Wall Street and the wealthy "elites" at the expense of the disenfranchised poor. This mythic framing set up Trump as the classic American hero. He—with unmistakable machismo—stood alone, taller and stronger than his foolish predecessors, finally fighting off the rich and powerful bad guys who were trying to exploit the town folk. He would save us by facing down the deep state. This framing was odd given that Trump had inherited a fortune and seemed to dispassionate observers more like a member of the moneyed elite than someone standing up to them.

Even before Trump was elected, his advisor Stephen Bannon published an article under a pseudonym explaining that Trump's election would unleash an epic battle between the lone champion and the elites' deep state. The underlying strategy was to make Trump appeal to people who dislike and distrust government, even though he actually was the government's head.

THE LIZARD MENACE

Around the time of the 2008 US presidential election, it was revealed that a lot of Democrats are really lizards. The goal of these lizards, like the Jews and the Illuminati and the deep state and other targets of conspiracy theorists, is world domination. "Lizard People" even made it onto the ballot in Minnesota, written in by a disgruntled voter who did not like any of the candidates. He later said it was intended as a joke, but there were those who were relieved by Republican gains in the 2010 midterm election, because this meant that the plot of lizards to take over the country had, at least for the moment, been foiled.

According to social media, lizards have the ability to change themselves into humans. David Icke, author of many lizard theories, claims that these lizards have been controlling human events since ancient times. Icke established his lizard theory with his 1998 book *The Biggest Secret* and promotes it in social media and his website.

Not all US lizards are Democrats. Among the lizards passing themselves off as human are Republicans George W. Bush (the former governor of Texas and US president) and Donald Rumsfeld (who served in the cabinets of both Bush presidents and died in 2021). Among Democrats, Bill and Hillary Clinton and Barack Obama are lizards. Queen Elizabeth, who claims no US party affiliation, is a lizard. Comedian Bob Hope was a lizard, as are contemporary celebrities Madonna, Katy Perry, and Angelina Jolie.

Icke claims that lizards are the force behind not only Freemasons but the Illuminati. People post theories on his website and elsewhere about how to spot a lizard person. According to the website Bump, telltale signs of a lizard person include green eyes, good eyesight and hearing, red hair, a love of space, low blood pressure, and—the biggest tell of all—a feeling of alienation from humanity. (I suppose there is some logic to suspecting that an alienated person is a lizard from outer space, but there are more likely explanations available.) Icke's forum suggests being wary of people whose bottom teeth show when they smile or whose eyes change size or have oddly large pupils. But someone self-identified as UFOchick cautioned that you can't always look for physical signs. "It's about the soul inhabiting the body, not the physical body," UFOchick warned.

These lizards are most likely from the Draco constellation, the eighth largest constellation, which, tellingly, is shaped like a dragon. But Sirius and Orion have not been ruled out as home to some of these lizards.

This in itself should ring warning bells. Perhaps it is overly harsh to call constellations a lie, but they are certainly a fantasy. Though still used by astronomers for purposes of mapping the night skies, they are not real locations in the universe. When it is said that something comes from a certain constellation, remember that a constellation is not an interstellar street address, and the stars of a constellation do not outline a neighborhood. Constellations are one of the oldest myths, probably dating back to prehistoric man. Ancient Sumerians, Egyptians, Chinese, Aboriginal Australians, and many others noted them. Stargazers with no understanding of science looked at stars and, by connecting dots, imagined various shapes. But if the same stars could be viewed from a vantage point far away from Earth, they would outline very different shapes. The stars of a constellation may appear to occupy a cluster, but in reality they are separated by vast interstellar distances. In most cases they have no relationship to one another apart from occupying the same galaxy, the Milky Way, and being bright enough to be seen with the naked eye from Earth.

You wouldn't need to be a constellation skeptic to doubt the claim that we are being invaded by lizards from outer space who are disguising themselves as human. But some people do believe this—constellations, lizards, and all. Public Policy Polling, a serious but not always reliable pollster, determined in April 2013 that 4 percent of Americans believe in lizard people, while another 7 percent were unsure. If true, this meant that about twelve million Americans are at least willing to entertain the possibility that lizard people exist. And probably there are more who think they exist but will not publicly acknowledge it for fear of retribution by lizard people.

FROM RUSSIA WITH LOVE – PART 2: THE CAMERA **TRACKS DOWN** THE MAIN STREET OF A QUAINT FISHING TOWN OFF THE **COAST OF MAINE**, THEN **MOVES THROUGH THE KITCHEN WINDOW** OF A SMALL HOUSE. INSIDE, WE SEE A YOUNG COUPLE NAMED **DICK AND JANE** SITTING AT A TABLE, **BROWSING THE INTERNET** ON THEIR PHONES.

LATER, DICK COMES ACROSS A BLOGGER NAMED **EMILY LOVE**, WHO HAS **TURNED AGAINST THE VACCINE**.

HER PHOTO AND BLOG POSTS MAKE EMILY SEEM LIKE **A WARM AND SINCERE PERSON**. SHE LIVES IN BOSTON AND TALKS TO NEW ENGLANDERS.

Hi! I'm Emily LOVE

JANE, YOU MIGHT BE RIGHT. THIS BLOGGER NAMED EMILY LOVE SEEMS LIKE AN HONEST PERSON, AND SHE'S WARNING US TO **BEWARE OF THE VACCINE**. SHE SAYS THERE'S **EVIDENCE** THAT IT'S **DANGEROUS**.

OH, AND SHE ALSO SAYS THAT RUSSIA IS BEING ATTACKED BY UKRAINIAN TERRORISTS.

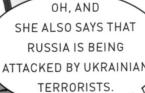

TO BE CONTINUED . . .

CHAPTER THREE

DENIAL: THE SHORT WAY around SCIENCE

"Of all discoveries and opinions, none may have exerted a greater effect on the human spirit than the doctrine of Copernicus. The world had scarcely become known as round and complete in itself when it was asked to waive the tremendous privilege of being the center of the universe. Never, perhaps, was a greater demand made on mankind—for, by this admission, so many things vanished in mist and smoke!"
—Johann Wolfgang von Goethe, *Theory of Colors*, 1810

The easiest ideas to absorb are intuitive ones that your senses tell you are correct.

It is easy to believe that spoiled food is bad to eat, because it looks and smells bad. We accept that water is good for plants because we see them flourish after a rain and wither in a drought. But people started to be confronted with science in the sixteenth century, and science is often unintuitive, sometimes even counterintuitive, contradicting the evidence of our senses.

A man or woman with no education and no knowledge of centuries of scientific learning might look around and conclude that our planet is flat. Of course, traveling far enough in any direction will return you to your starting place, which proves that Earth is round, not flat, but who travels that far? It certainly looks flat, and that is good enough for many people.

Science tells us that Earth rotates. If you stand still at the equator you are spinning around Earth's axis at 1,000 miles per hour (460 meters per second), but nothing in your senses tells you that you are moving at all. It is just something you have been told. Looking up, you can plainly see the sun moving across the sky, and you must accept the word of science that what you are seeing is not the sun orbiting Earth but Earth spinning. In fact, science tells us that Earth orbits the sun—not the other way around—and the speed of that orbit is 67,000 miles per hour (30

Greek geographers figured out that Earth is spherical in the third century BCE, yet some today still believe in a flat Earth. Some think Earth is a disk contained by a wall of ice around the rim. Flat-Earthers reject "scientism" and say that photos of the spherical Earth seen from space are faked. This conspiracy theory attracts fewer believers than many others; a 2017 poll by Public Policy Polling found that only 1 percent of Americans believed the Earth was flat, with an additional 6 percent saying they weren't sure.

kilometers per second)—or 584 million miles a year. That is hard to believe, but science has proven it.

Meanwhile our solar system—the sun, Earth, and the other planets—is orbiting around the center of the Milky Way galaxy at 490,000 miles per hour (220 kilometers per second), and the Milky Way galaxy is hurtling through space at more than 2 million miles per hour (1,000 kilometers per second).

When you finish this sentence, you'll be 6,000 miles from where you were when you began it. Feeling dizzy yet?

When someone falls ill, nothing is seen attacking the victim, so it is natural to blame some intangible evil spirit. Most educated people by the seventeenth century had stopped blaming the devil for diseases, and by the late nineteenth century it became clear that some illnesses were caused by germs so small they could not be seen with the naked eye. And yet, if you don't have a microscope, what evidence of this do you have? For centuries it was believed that an illness could be removed with magnets. Many people who do not have a microscope *do* have a magnet, and magnetism is a force whose effects they can see even if they can't understand.

Most of the great treatises that have reshaped our view of the world are incomprehensible to most of us. We believe the essential theories of Copernicus, Galileo, Newton, and Einstein but have never read their books; if we attempted to read them, we could not make sense of them.

They are written for people with science and math skills far beyond what most of us can claim. We do not understand Einstein's theory of relativity, but most of us don't doubt it. Nor do most of us possess the math skills by which Newton explained gravity, yet we have no doubt that gravity is real.

Science often seems beyond us. We read of this year's Nobel Prize winner for physics and scratch our heads. If we are honest, we have no idea what this scientist accomplished. Most physics today is about quantum mechanics, the creation of particles. It is the study of how the universe operates at a level smaller than an atom. Arithmetic, geometry, algebra, calculus (which Newton invented three centuries ago), differential equations, matrix algebra, group theory—mastering these skills will get us to college physics, but to understand today's research we have to go beyond even that. Commenting on the eighteenth-century debates about gravity and the laws of motion, Voltaire quipped that according to Descartes and the French, "everything is done by an impulsion that nobody understands," whereas with Newton, "it is by an attraction, the cause of which is not better known."

So there seems to be a leap of faith in *believing* science, but actually there is not. Religious people who think that science has dismantled the underpinnings of religion make the mistake of seeing science as an alternative faith. Our beliefs are better than yours, they claim. But while religion asks you to believe—to accept an idea on faith—science does the opposite. Science is about testing and retesting an idea to prove that it is right. As soon as a theory is established, other scientists rush to prove it wrong. The best scientific discoveries hold up to repeated testing, while many others are proven wrong.

The strength of science is this eternal, self-doubting allowance for the possibility of a mistake. It is this habit of doubt and **constant testing** that makes scientific thinking the greatest defense against lying.

For centuries there has been the semblance of a debate between religion and science, but in truth they cannot debate because they speak different languages and think in different ways. One side believes and one side doubts. Though Galileo Galilei has been called the father of

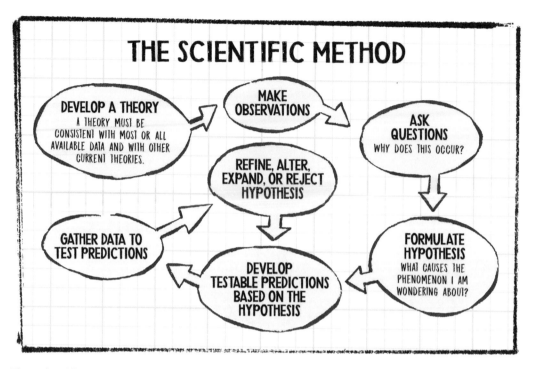

THE SCIENTIFIC METHOD

DEVELOP A THEORY
A THEORY MUST BE CONSISTENT WITH MOST OR ALL AVAILABLE DATA AND WITH OTHER CURRENT THEORIES.

MAKE OBSERVATIONS

ASK QUESTIONS
WHY DOES THIS OCCUR?

REFINE, ALTER, EXPAND, OR REJECT HYPOTHESIS

GATHER DATA TO TEST PREDICTIONS

DEVELOP TESTABLE PREDICTIONS BASED ON THE HYPOTHESIS

FORMULATE HYPOTHESIS
WHAT CAUSES THE PHENOMENON I AM WONDERING ABOUT?

The scientific method as a cyclical process of questioning, testing, and continuous improvement.

observational astronomy, he made a number of erroneous observations about the moon through his crude telescope, seeing large bodies of water that aren't there and measuring lunar mountains far higher than they actually are. Newton demonstrated that, contrary to Galileo's studies, the moon *does* influence tides. Newton did not merely believe this; he demonstrated it. For centuries scientists looked for flaws in Newton's discoveries. Einstein, in one of his most important discoveries, showed that if the speed of a particle is high enough, Newton's calculations do not work. This does not dispose of Newton's discoveries any more than Newton disposed of Galileo's work. It is simply fine tuning.

Copernicus, Galileo, Newton, and Darwin all made mistakes, and physicists are looking for chinks in Einstein's theory of relativity, though it has held up well. Despite some mistakes, these geniuses provided building blocks to our understanding of the universe.

Science challenges religion—its political power, its intellectual standing, and its assumptions on how the universe works. Science removed heaven from the skies and replaced it with space. It replaced an active, all-seeing God who controls events with a series of natural laws that carry out their functions blindly.

A law of nature will always act in the same way, regardless of what we do or believe. Germs rather than God determine who is healthy and who is sick, and they can be fought off because they are predictable.

Sometimes science is only challenging legends of the Bible that many religious people do not take literally. But for those who do take them literally, science is a problem. The Swedish biologist Carolus Linnaeus attempted to identify and name all the species of the plant and animal kingdoms. By 1740, when he had named 5,600 species—a fraction of what is known today—he questioned what kind of boat Noah could have had to hold all those organisms.

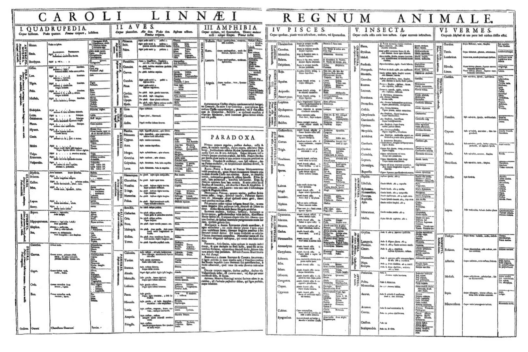

A taxonomy of the animal kingdom, from the first (1735) edition of *Systema Naturae*, by Carolus Linnaeus.

A fissure between science and religion formed from the beginning of science. Religious people today who see science as the enemy live with contradictions. They operate their televisions with remote controls, use social media on their computers and cell phones, drive cars with sophisticated electronics, and take antibiotics. Though opposed to science, they enjoy its benefits. The use of the technology of social media to denounce science is a fundamental contradiction.

At a book fair in Frankfort, Kentucky, a woman told me she had read one of my books and wanted to know why I believed in climate change. I told her that it is not a question of belief, that scientists have amassed unassailable evidence about how climate change is happening. "You talk to scientists?" she asked. When I said that I did, she did not conceal her disdain.

Most people
who deny science and despise scientists
are just picking and choosing
which science to ignore
and which to enjoy.

SCIENTIFIC LIES

Of course, there are bad scientists, too—scientists who don't just make mistakes but pursue malicious agendas. There are scientists who deny climate change, despite overwhelming evidence, because they are promoting energy companies that cause it. Sometimes they are simply lying. The oil company Exxon did studies proving climate change. The scientists were honest, but then the company lied and denied their own science. US Congressional hearings in late 2021 revealed that such intentional disinformation about climate change is a common practice among the leading oil companies.

Science with an agenda is usually bad science. One of the greatest lies in history was promoted by bad science. How could slavery and the colonization of Africa be justified unless Black people were somehow inferior? Thomas Jefferson, who proudly identified himself as a scientist (the only US president apart from Jimmy Carter to do so), engaged in legitimate scientific inquiries, especially in agriculture. He had telescopes and automatic doors at his home, Monticello, and he mastered the writings of Newton. But in his only book, the 1781 *Notes on the State of Virginia*, he proclaimed that Black people are not as attractive as white people and are of lower intelligence. He wrote that not a single Black "could be found capable of tracing and comprehending the investigations of Euclid, and that in imagination they are dull, tasteless, and anomalous." He did not seem to think they could be overworked, since they required less sleep than white people. There it is: America's founding scientist.

African American slaves had the pseudoscience of their biological inferiority pounded into them. Louis Agassiz (1807–1873), a Swiss-born biologist and geologist who studied fossils, rejected Darwin's ideas of evolution and insisted that the natural order had been arranged by a divine plan. From his position at Harvard University, he was well-known for his attempts to popularize the sciences while rejecting important new ideas. He was an advocate of polygenism, a bogus scientific position (what is known today as a pseudoscience) claiming that different races had biologically different origins. Based on this, he argued for the inferiority of Black people and the importance of not mixing the races. He collected photographs of slaves to demonstrate their inferiority, although these photos, the first ever taken of slaves, seemed to argue that slaves were not inferior but malnourished and mistreated. By the end of his life his reputation was considerably diminished, not because of his racism but because of his stubborn and unscientific opposition to the work of Darwin. He said he had never realized how quickly Darwinism would become accepted. He had not expected leading scientists to embrace it.

It has been a popular misconception that the science pioneers who caused this revolution fought against religion. Religion often fought against them, but they were mostly religious people. Francis Bacon, one of the first scientific thinkers, believed that what scientists were learning demonstrated the significance of God's creation. Robert Boyle, the so-called father of chemistry, and Isaac Newton, the founding physicist, both believed that the laws of matter they were beginning to understand were proof of the existence of God. Newton said of his laws of motion that "the motions which the planets now have could not spring from any natural Cause alone but were impressed by an intelligent agent." Boyle was so concerned that science might turn people away from religion that in 1691 he left in his will fifty pounds annually for lectures in support of

Christianity and to combat atheism. The Catholic Church condemned Galileo to life imprisonment (later house arrest) for teaching the ideas of Copernicus, but neither Copernicus nor Galileo was anti-church.

Charles Darwin was considering a career as an Anglican minister when he formulated the ideas on evolution that continue to upset some religious people to this day.

In 1543, when Copernicus's book was published, few read it and even fewer understood it. To those who did understand it, he demonstrated that our concept of the universe was wrong. Earth and its beings were not the central accomplishment of the universe but one of many planets that revolved around the sun. Other planets were doing the exact same thing. Andreas Osiander, a Lutheran theologian, wrote a preface that Copernicus never approved, saying that, of course, this was all foolishness and there was no need to believe it. Initially there was little church objection. Humans and Earth were the center of the universe, and Copernicus was an insignificant crackpot.

It is ironic that Copernicus's book about astronomy, *On the Revolutions of Celestial Bodies,* is the first known use of the word "revolution" in a non-astronomical sense; by revolution he meant a returning of things to their proper order, both literally and metaphorically. A natural order would unfold with or without the interference of humans, he believed. He did not write of or desire revolution in the modern sense, yet his ideas did create a revolution.

When people started to believe it, this scarcely read book shook the world as few books have. If Earth is not the center of the universe but just one of numerous balls circling the sun, all of them operating under the same laws of motion, then we are considerably less special, and there is no heaven anchored to Earth.

Nicolaus Copernicus was born in Poland in 1473 and educated in Renaissance Italy. He never wanted to be a revolutionary; he was a conservative, churchgoing man and even launched his book in a little-known cathedral. He had established a room for astronomic observation in the cathedral and passed out his writings about a solar-centered universe for years before ever publishing the theory. He said that the appearance of stars orbiting around Earth was an optical illusion caused by the spinning of Earth. He died shortly after his masterpiece was published and may not ever have seen it with the unwanted preface.

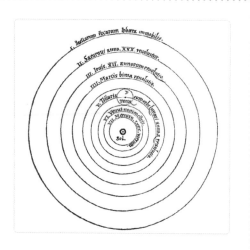

Copernicus published this model of the universe in 1543, placing the sun at the center, motionless, with the planets circling around it at uniform speeds. It was closer to the truth than the Earth-centered model but has been continuously improved by subsequent scientific discoveries. That's how science works.

Galileo Galilei was a much larger personality and paid a price for that. He is remembered as the symbol of the conflict between science and religion. He was born in Pisa in 1564, the year Michelangelo died and Shakespeare was born. His oddly repetitive name reflects the tradition in his native Tuscany of naming the first-born son with the family name for a first name. As a student he was drawn to geometry, and after twenty years he was able to give the correct law of motion to falling objects, the beginning of an understanding of how the world worked. In 1609 he learned of a device built by a Flemish optician for studying distant objects. Soon he built his own telescope and started studying what used to be called the heavens.

He described his observations of the moon, Jupiter and its four moons, and numerous stars. Later he studied Venus. To the disapproval of the church, he announced his acceptance of the solar system as described by Copernicus, affirming that Earth and the other planets spin on their axes and revolve around the sun. This got much more of a reaction, both positive and negative, than when Copernicus had described the same thing.

Galileo could prove it. Artists, writers, and freethinkers supported him, while he was attacked by most established scholars. In 1616 the church banned the writings of Copernicus and ordered Galileo to stop defending Copernicus's theory.

Galileo, unlike Copernicus, was arrogant and made enemies easily. **He did not defend the Bible;** he said that where it conflicts with mathematical science, it needed to be rewritten. **He joked that the Bible tells us how to go to heaven** but not how the heavens go.

Many who understood his work thought he was foolish to take on the established powers, but he asked, "Who would set a limit to the mind of man? Who would dare assert that we know all there is to be known?" And so, Galileo became a martyr for science, a symbol of the new Enlightenment taking on the old ways.

Isaac Newton, an Englishman born in December 1642, only months after Galileo's death, explained "the laws of motion" by which objects small and large moved. He explained the force of gravity, why things fall. He invented calculus, which gave him the mathematics to prove his theories. He also demonstrated that "white light" contains all colors and can be broken down to the colors of the rainbow.

Few have read his work, and even fewer understand it, but he explained how the world we live in works. Even today, with a few revisions from Einstein, our understanding of the world and of science is Newtonian. Quantum mechanics and how a moon landing arrives at the right spot (unless you think the moon landing is a hoax) are rooted in Newton.

And yet Newton was not controversial. He was a national hero in England and widely admired throughout Europe. When he died in March 1727, he was buried in Westminster Abbey, and an enormous monument was built. Monuments and medals were created all over Europe to honor the man who was and still is considered "England's greatest genius."

By Newton's time, men of science were becoming heroes. Science was growing, and religion was declining. While there were ever fewer churches, a trend that continues today, there were more and more scientific societies. Between 1600 and 1793, more than seventy official science societies were established around the world.

Charles Darwin, on the other hand, met considerable opposition in his own time and still does today. This may be because he is easier to understand. Most science deniers lack a vocabulary to refute a Newton or an Einstein, but Darwin's books are readable.

START HERE

IGNORE THE EVIDENCE OF YOUR SENSES JUMP AHEAD 3 SPACES

QUIT SCHOOL MOVE TO THE HEAD OF THE CLASS 3 SPACES

FALL OFF THE EDGE OF THE EARTH CLIMB BACK UP AND START OVER

BLAME THE ELITES ADVANCE 2 SPACES

YOU WIN! DO ANYTHING YOU WANT!

ALIENS PROBE YOUR BODY FLY AHEAD 3 SPACES

YOUR BROTHER GOT THE VACCINE NOW HE HAS A CHIP IN HIS BUTT FALL BACK 2 SPACES

DENIAL!

WHO NEEDS SCIENCE WHEN YOU HAVE DENIAL?!

THE SHORT WAY AROUND SCIENCE GAME!

ATTACK SOMEONE ON SOCIAL MEDIA RAGE AHEAD ONE SPACE

EVOLUTION IS A LIE! CRAWL AHEAD 1 SPACE

BURN A BOOK WHO READS, ANYWAY?

PROVE COVID IS FAKE GO AHEAD 2 SPACES

IF CLIMATE CHANGE IS REAL, WHY IS IT SNOWING? MOVE AHEAD 2 SPACES

REFUSE TO GET THE VACCINE YOU'RE FREE! MARCH AHEAD 1 SPACE

INCLUDES **4 "HEAD IN THE SAND" GAME PIECES**

Essentially, he said that the web of life is the outcome of a struggle for survival in which species with successful strategies live on and continue to evolve, while others become extinct. Success or failure depends on natural selection; the species with the best strategies have the best chances to survive and reproduce. This mechanism requires no ongoing intervention from God.

You don't need calculus to see how natural selection works. Darwin's books—*On the Origin of Species, The Descent of Man,* and *Voyage of the Beagle*—are all understandable, even enjoyable science books in which he explains how he arrived at his ideas.

Religious people who oppose Darwin say to this day that he lacked proof. But not only did he provide a great deal of proof, but most every discovery in biology for the past 150 years, including genetics and DNA, show that Darwin was right. Part of the evidence he pointed to was fossils. In a group of fossils, it becomes clear that the fossilized organisms lived and died at different times. Fossils found close to the ground surface are similar to modern species, but very different variations are found in deeper strata. It became clear that some of these fossils were the remains of extinct species.

One of the religious arguments against this clear evidence is that fossils were placed on earth by the devil in order to deceive us. If you refute this argument, you are showing yourself to be an agent of the devil. It is not belief in God but belief in the devil that blocks knowledge.

Such arguments

lead to a culture of lying in which demagogues and conspiracy theorists can thrive, a culture in which facts no longer matter. You can declare anything to be true if no proof is required.

As president, Donald Trump told his followers that what they were hearing, seeing, and reading was not what was happening. In other words, the facts you hear are just intended to deceive you. Disregard the truth, and instead listen to me.

ATLANTIS: THE OLDEST LIVING LIE

The Age of Enlightenment caused a decline in magicians, but by the late nineteenth century a new breed started finding popular support. Perhaps people were missing the simplicity of magic. These magicians were not anti-science. They claimed that their work was based on science, though scientists did not agree. They claimed to be going beyond science to explain things science was missing. They said that they were investigating "the paranormal"—psychic, mental, or spiritual phenomena that were not normal but were nonetheless real.

Some of these parapsychologists were sincere, dedicated researchers. Others were frauds and con artists. But they were all documenting things that had no scientific support.

"Spiritists" claimed to communicate with the dead and saw themselves as expanding the realm of science. The movement was internationally popular in the nineteenth century and retained a strong following into the twentieth. Sincere spiritists who began exposing fraudulent fellow practitioners became known as "the Skeptics."

"New Agers" of the late 1960s and early 1970s aimed to disrupt "the establishment" and create a better society. More leftist than rightist, they drew their ranks from antiwar protesters, Black Power advocates, feminists, hippies, and people living in communes—the largely disillusioned "counterculture" of the 1960s. Constructing their beliefs from a mixture of science, astrology, psychology, and Eastern and Native American world views, they predicted the coming of a new age of greater wisdom and understanding, "The Age of Aquarius," as alluded to in a hit song from the 1968 rock musical *Hair*, "Aquarius/Let the Sun Shine In." The lyrics promised an age of "harmony and understanding, sympathy and trust abounding / no more falsehoods or derisions / golden living dreams of visions / mystic crystal revelation / and the mind's true liberation / Aquarius!"

Note the "mystic crystal revelation." In the 1980s and 1990s, the Skeptics tried to separate New Agers from some of their more scientifically dubious beliefs such as crystal healing, a field that Skeptics believed was filled with charlatans. Crystal healing was popularized by Katrina Raphaell's 1985 book *Crystal Enlightenment*. The title, implying an improvement on the Enlightenment, is typically New Age.

Raphaell began in solid science—geology—discussing how various crystals are mined, cut, and polished. Then she went on to explain that crystals contain the ancient wisdom of Atlantis, a continent with a highly advanced civilization that sank in one day and one night. The existence of Atlantis was revealed by the ancient Greek philosopher Plato, who believed in the usefulness of a lie in a good cause. If, as Aristotle and others suggested, Plato was lying about Atlantis, it is one of the world's oldest lies. Aristotle said of Plato, "He could create nations out of thin air and then destroy them."

Scientists studying plate tectonics, the evolution of the continents and ocean beds, say there is no place in Earth's jigsaw-puzzle crust for a vanished continent, yet it keeps being discovered in places as diverse as Bolivia, Turkey, Antarctica, and the Caribbean. Plato himself was clear about Atlantis's location in the Atlantic Ocean, but there is nothing there. In 1702, Olaus Rudbeck, a Swedish scientist dismissed by his colleagues as a quack, published a 3,000-page work showing that Sweden was the original Atlantis.

Rudbeck is certainly no harder to believe than Katrina Raphaell, who asserted that Atlantis was destroyed because its rarefied knowledge was abused and misused. But before it was destroyed, uncorrupted wise ones preserved the knowledge in crystals.

Some thought crystals might contain the power of healing, or meditative powers leading to ancient wisdom, or the souls of ancient Native Americans. These theories had to be true, according to supporters; otherwise, why did advanced civilizations in Tibet, Egypt, and Latin America all construct pyramids like the tips of crystals?

Even the most committed New Agers admit that crystals offer a tremendous opportunity for fraud. Special crystals, some made of cheap glass, are widely sold. "Crystal therapy" is available. In 2021, for $28.94, you could buy online a set of four crystals that would help the autistic balance left- and right-brain activity. For $25.46 you could buy a crystal bead bracelet that provided "strength to overcome addictions." A "beginner's Crystal Kit" was available for $39.95.

Darwin's ideas were eventually accepted and admired by scientists and educated people around the world, but the anti-Darwin movement survives to this day. It is based largely on ignorance of what Darwin was saying, misguided notions that he was attacking the Bible and saying that humans are really monkeys. A number of laws passed in the United States in the early twentieth century prohibited the teaching of evolution in public schools. The state of Tennessee passed such a law in 1925, naming it after farmer and Christian activist John W. Butler.

There are two important insights into science denial here. The first is that Butler admitted to having no idea what evolution was but had heard that children were coming home from school denying the Bible. Science deniers often do not understand the science they are denying.

The second insight is that the governor who signed the legislation into law, Austin Peay, had no interest in the anti-evolution cause and no intention of enforcing the law or interfering with school curricula. He signed it simply to get the support of rural politicians and voters. That is often the goal of science-denying politicians.

The law became famous because the American Civil Liberties Union challenged its legality. William Jennings Bryan, a three-time US presidential nominee, represented the anti-evolution side, and Clarence Darrow, the most famous trial lawyer in America, represented the pro-evolution side. The ACLU was unable to find a biology teacher to stand up for the cause, but John Scopes, a math and science teacher who privately confessed that he could not recall if he had ever taught evolution, volunteered. He was convicted and fined $100, but his conviction was reversed on appeal. After the Scopes trial, numerous states tried but failed to pass similar laws. The law was not repealed until 1967; the following year, the Supreme Court ruled such teaching bans unconstitutional. Some states, however, continue to encourage the teaching of creationism

The Scopes trial made headlines around the country, including this *Washington Times* front page on July 20, 1925. The article noted that the eight scientists assembled by the defense were allowed to submit written evidence but not to testify in court.

and intelligent design (creationism with a scientific patina) alongside evolution as an equally plausible theory.

Recent polls suggest that 18 to 40 percent of the US public are creationists, while 45 percent believe in evolution. Many do not even know what evolution is. In most other countries, a clear majority of people accept evolution.

Both the Bible and the Qur'an seem to say that the Earth is flat.

Since this is easy to disprove, most followers have turned to a less literal interpretation. But in recent decades the chief Islamic religious authority in Saudi Arabia, Sheikh Abdul Aziz Ibn Baz, a blind cleric who tried to strengthen the power of the ruling family, issued a decree, a *fatwa,* that Earth is flat and anyone who says otherwise is denying God and should be punished.

Stephen Hawking, a leading theoretical physicist, argued that science and religion are attempting to answer the same questions.

He said there will always be some who prefer religion though, "because it gives comfort, and they do not trust or understand science."

A 2008 Pew Research Center showed that 60 percent of American adults believe that God is a person with whom a believer can have a relationship. An overwhelming majority of working scientists, on the other hand—unlike Copernicus, Galileo, Newton, and Darwin—do not believe in the existence of a personal God looking after us. If they are honest scientists, they don't believe in belief. To a scientist, the path to truth is to formulate a theory and test it. Since there is no way to test the existence of God, there is no way for a scientist to accept or reject religion. I asked the late Edward Osborne Wilson, a leading evolutionary biologist, if he thought God existed. His perfect scientific answer was, "I have no way of knowing." A scientist may refute certain beliefs as provably wrong, but to refute the existence of God is as unscientific as refuting science.

Today many scientists subcribe to the idea that a concentration of space and temperature expanded to create the universe. It is called the Big Bang, which is a misnomer because it was not an explosion but a steady expansion. Many physicists believe that this, and not the will of God, created the universe. Even if this is true, it does not explain where the concentration of space and temperature came from, so God remains for those who want him (or her, or it).

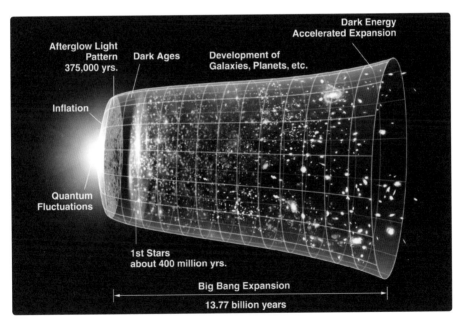

An artist's timeline of the evolution of the universe since the Big Bang 13.77 billion years ago, including (at left) the early period of exponential growth known as "inflation." The height of the grid represents the size of the universe through time.

The scientist may say that the laws of nature operate on their own and are not controlled by a god, but that does not answer the question, how did these laws come about? Yiddish novelist Isaac Bashevis Singer, not a particularly religious man, wrote, "Modern man was as fanatic in his non-belief as ancient man had been in his faith."

Certainly there is no way to disprove the existence of God, but that does not mean that scientifically proven theories can logically be refuted. It took more than 300 years for the Catholic Church to admit that Galileo was right and to clear his name of heresy in 1992. By the end of the twentieth century, however, the Catholic consensus supported a concept of "theistic evolution"—i.e., that God created the universe in which cosmic and biological evolution have occurred. Many Evangelicals reject this, continuing to insist on a literal interpretation of the Bible.

Who will believe a politician who declares that climate change is a hoax?

Of course he or she is supported by coal-mining and oil companies who produce enormous amounts of carbon. But with glaciers melting, catastrophic changes in the weather, and the unraveling of the ocean food chain, who—if they're being honest with themselves—would not know they are being lied to? Islands and shorelines are vanishing under a rising sea. Climate change can be seen plainly and in many ways.

The truth is that most Americans lack the science proficiency to challenge science liars. Ever fewer Americans have a solid grounding in science and mathematics, the very fields that give people the tools to analyze, test, and see through lies. Liars don't generally target scientists. They aim at people who have no science background.

In truth, it is far easier to deny science than to understand it.

Studies have indicated that a huge majority of Americans (as much as 95 percent of the population) are "science illiterate," though the definition of science literacy can be debated. The US government has disparaged science and science education since 1980, when Ronald Reagan ran for president with a promise of eliminating the Department of Education. He said in his 1967 campaign for governor of California, "Why should we subsidize intellectual curiosity?"

In 1995, after Republicans took control of Congress, they closed the Office of Technology Assessment, saying that it cost too much and was anti-Republican. (The claim that a scientific body is anti-Republican says something about the modern Republican Party.) The OTA was a group of scientists charged with advising the US Congress on matters of science. It was needed because, like most of their constituents, few members of Congress have any science background.

Testing has shown that 63 percent of American adults do not know that dinosaurs became extinct before human beings appeared. Seventy-five percent of adult Americans do not know that antibiotics kill bacteria, though most will take an antibiotic if prescribed. Fifty-seven percent do not know that electrons are smaller than atoms. About half of Americans do not know of the Copernican universe and still think the sun revolves around Earth. These are the people who are most susceptible to lies, or to what right-wing political operatives sometimes call "alternative facts." If a cynical politician wants to establish a cult following, the trick is to create a different reality, a world of so-called facts that belong exclusively to members of the cult. Let others refute them if they can.

It's faster to create lies
than to refute them. The fact-checkers are always playing catchup.

An anonymous source in the George W. Bush administration scoffed at people who believe that solutions emerge from a judicious study of discernible reality. "That's not the way the world really works anymore," he or she told reporter Ron Suskind in 2004. "We're an empire now, and when we act, we create our own reality. And while you're studying that reality—judiciously, as you will—we'll act again, creating other new realities, which you can study too, and that's how things will sort out. We're history's actors . . . and you, all of you, will be left to just study what we do."

This idea that an alternative reality could be offered as a different truth was well established by the time Donald Trump assumed the US presidency in 2017. His staff spoke openly of it, no longer bothering to remain anonymous. When White House Press Secretary Sean Spicer made blatantly false and easily disprovable claims about the size of the turnout for the 2017 presidential inauguration, obvious lies in support of Trump's obvious lies, former campaign manager Kellyanne Conway explained that Spicer was just giving alternative facts—a different set of facts for those who preferred them.

When you hear things that are obviously lies, you need to understand that they are not necessarily intended for you.

VACCINES: A SHOT IN THE DARK

*"A lie will gallop halfway round the world before
the truth has time to pull its breeches on."*

This quote itself has a telling history. Sometimes with breeches, sometimes with pants, and sometimes with shoes, it has been attributed to Mark Twain, Winston Churchill, and Cordell Hull, who was Franklin Roosevelt's secretary of state. It is probably attributed to a few others as well, because once a good quote starts gathering multiple attributions, there is no end to it. The point being made is that a successful lie never completely dies and is extremely hard to stop with the truth

No matter how many decades of studies accumulate showing that vaccines do not cause autism, and no matter the complete absence of medical research indicating that they do, anti-vaxxers still believe the myths of harm. Numerous studies by reputable sources, including the federal government's Centers for Disease Control, show that there is no link between childhood vaccines and autism. The National Academy of Medicine, an independent nonprofit, analyzed more than 1,000 research papers before reaching the same conclusion in 2011.

Thiomersal is a mercury-containing preservative used in vaccines when several doses are taken from the same vial. Although the form of mercury used has low toxicity, the CDC and the American Academy of Pediatrics, as part of a broad effort to reduce mercury in children, asked manufacturers to stop using thiomersal. Anti-vaxxers concluded from this that the preservative was removed due to its role in spreading autism. That is not the case. Several studies have shown no link between thiomersal and autism, and the preservative's removal has done nothing to reduce the spread of autism, but the myth lives on.

It is sometimes believed that the combination of vaccines given to children—measles, mumps, rubella, and flu—causes autism, but when this was studied it was found that vaccines introduce only a tiny fraction of the pathogens a child encounters, and the human immune system can withstand thousands of vaccines.

Such reassuring studies have been published in leading scientific journals, where they have been peer-reviewed by other scientists prior to publication. A scientist needs credentials to be published in such journals, but there are other journals in which almost anyone can publish without peer review, and these are the journals where studies showing the link between vaccine and autism are found. Later, under scrutiny, they are sometimes withdrawn. Sometimes they are discredited by the World Health Organization, which is what happened to the work of Canadian ophthalmology professor Christopher Shaw. His work was shown to have been funded by an anti-vaccination group, the Dwoskin Family Foundation. But by the time such articles are discredited, they have often been reported in the mainstream press and become another lie that galloped halfway around the world.

The alleged link between vaccines and autism appears to have originated with a fraudulent 1998 study by a British physician, Andrew Wakefield, that appeared in *The Lancet*, a respected, peer-reviewed medical journal. *The London Sunday Times* reported on how data had been misreported. *The British Medical Journal* showed how the study had been falsified to get the result Wakefield was looking for. The first tip-off should have been how small his sample size was. He only looked at twelve children. *The British Medical Journal* said that this study could not have been explained simply by incompetence; there was a clear "intent to deceive." Wakefield was lying. It was later shown that at the time of the study, he received more than £400,000 (well over a half-million dollars) from a lawyer working on a lawsuit against vaccine manufacturers. Wakefield was stripped of his medical license. *The Lancet* retracted the article in 2010, twelve years after publishing it.

The supposed link between vaccines and autism is actually an old conspiracy theory, almost as old as vaccines themselves. Right-wing anti-vaxxers blame a list of culprits including government and the medical establishment. Left-wing anti-vaxxers suspect big pharmaceutical companies. *The Protocols of the Elders of Zion*, a famous antisemitic tract, warns that inoculating against diseases is a Jewish plot.

The studies claiming links to autism have all been frauds, disproved over and over again, yet those who still cling to the myth include actor Robert De Niro (who is motivated by an autistic son), actor/comedian Jim Carrey, and comedian/commentator Bill Maher, who presents himself as an antivaccine agnostic. He asks, "How do you know there is no connection?," when in reality there is a mountain of thorough studies to answer that question. "We don't know a lot about how the body works. So how do vaccines fit in with, I don't know, all the new chemicals?" he asks, but in fact we do know a lot about how the body works. That is how vaccines were developed to prevent disease, and even Maher admits that they do work. He is a television celebrity trying to tap into an anti-science public, sneeringly referring to doctors as "people in the white coats."

Donald Trump, never one to pass up on a malicious lie, said in a 2015 presidential debate that he personally knew a two-year-old who had recently received a combined vaccine, developed a tremendous fever, and become autistic. He never identified this child.

Rescuing children from harm is always an effective way to draw followers to a conspiracy theory, only in this case it is the people opposing vaccines who are harming children. Diseases such as measles and whooping cough were completely conquered in the twentieth century but are now coming back, thanks to undefeatable liars and crackpots—a deadly conspiracy theory.

CHAPTER FOUR

FAVORITE LIES about WOMEN

It is not unreasonable that this scum of humanity should be drawn chiefly from the feminine sex.
—Nicholas Rémy, 1595, French judge who sentenced 800 people to death for witchcraft

Witchcraft was a lie directed against women.

Some historians argue that this is an oversimplification, and it is true that in a few places—Iceland, Finland, Estonia, and Russia—men were commonly accused as well. Records show, however, that between 75 and 85 percent of the accused were women, and in most places it was predominantly women who were executed as witches. It is also argued that many of the accusers were themselves women, and this is tragically true. Like men, they invented "eyewitness" accounts of women seen consorting with the devil. Sometimes the accuser's motive was to settle an old grudge, but more often the accuser had herself been accused and was trying to save her own life by testifying against others. Confessions were often obtained by torture. Many of the judges and prosecutors, like Nicolas Rémy, made clear their animosity toward women.

It was the peasantry—not the church or aristocracy—who believed in witchcraft in the Middle Ages. In 787 AD, Charlemagne, the powerful future emperor of most of Western Europe, outlawed the execution of those accused of being witches. The penalty for executing a supposed witch was death. In the tenth century, the Catholic Church required its clergy to preach against the belief in witches.

But this backward and mostly forgotten belief reemerged in the fifteenth century, when women were accused of consorting with the devil, flying through the air, and plotting against society. Witch trials began in the western Alpine region of France and Switzerland and spread throughout Europe and eventually to North America. By the time the mass delusion waned in the seventeenth century, as many as 100,000 people, mostly women, had been put to horrific deaths for consorting with the devil. Most had been tied to a stake and set on fire.

The title page of a 1613 pamphlet in England shows a suspected witch being dunked in a river. Her thumbs appear to be bound, as was sometimes done.

The myth of witchcraft took root in the intersection of belief in the devil with belief in the inferiority of women. Because they are less intelligent than men, it was thought, women are more easily tricked by the devil. Also, women can be seduced by the devil because they are slaves to their passions. "The Devil uses them because he knows that women love carnal pleasures," Judge Rémy proclaimed. The accuser sometimes seemed to be motivated by sexual jealousy or frustration. A woman had to be careful whose advances she spurned.

Accusations from other women might also be motivated by jealousy. Allegations of having witnessed satanic rituals and dark magic were clearly malicious lies, but a well-placed lie could get a woman burned alive. Prominent husbands or sons saved a few wives and mothers, but most women, once accused, found no way out.

How could you prove that you were not in league with the devil? Some were tied up and thrown in cold water. If they drowned, they were declared innocent, but those who floated were clearly witches and were then burned at the stake.

In the 1530s, hundreds of women were convicted of witchcraft and burned in Denmark. Witch trials in Europe reached their height between 1560 and 1630, coinciding with a series of religious wars. In 1587, in the German town of Trier, 368 people were executed, mostly women. Seventy people were convicted of witchcraft and burned in Scotland in 1590 because bad weather hampered Scottish King James IV's voyage to Denmark to collect his bride.

Often witches were scapegoats for bad weather, disease outbreaks, or crop failures. Often they were accused by peasants for very local reasons. If a tree stopped bearing fruit, perhaps the witch living next door had caused this by whistling.

In the seventeenth century, after Catholics regained control from Protestants in southern Germany, the region saw wholesale slaughter. In Bamberg, Germany, 300 alleged witches were executed. Julius Echter von Mespelbrunn, Bishop of Würzberg, burned to death 900 men, women, and children in his eight years in power. Noblemen, government officials, priests, and vagrants were charged with singing songs of the devil, practicing satanic rituals, or having sex with the devil and were summarily executed.

Sexual humiliation was often part of the persecution of women. Sometimes they were stripped naked and completely shaved, then their bodies were examined inch by inch and pricked here and there with a pin. If a spot was found that didn't bleed, that was the spot of the devil.

In the beginning of the seventeenth century, there was widespread concern among the Basque people of the mountains of northern Navarre that women were rubbing ointment on their skin and flying through the air to secret witch meetings. Here, as in many other places and times, the sexual component was clear. It was said that witches participated in mass orgies with the devil or flew into fields for group sex with billy goats. A commission established to interrogate suspected witches asked them such questions as do you have to fly to a witch meeting or are there other ways to get there?

The underlying premise— that the accused were in fact witches who were conspiring together— went unchallenged.

One popular explanation for why women became witches was that they ate a lot of apples and drank apple cider. Apples and apple cider are staples in the mountainous Basque country, but an ample consumption of apples by women was significant because, after all, Eve betrayed Adam with an apple, so apples are a woman's weapon against men. Do you think this might be sexist?

Rural Basques were arrested by the hundreds, and by 1609 French administrators were involved, with some French officials claiming that most Basque women were witches. The hysteria lasted only a few years, but an estimated six hundred Basques, mostly women, were burned to death in that time.

That the witch hysteria spread to colonial Massachusetts in 1692 is odd, because by then belief in witches had faded in Europe, where it was remembered as an unfortunate mass delusion of a generation or two earlier. But the late seventeenth century was not a good time in Massachusetts. The colonies had not recovered from the First Indian War, sometimes called King Philip's War, after the English name for the chief of the Wampanoags, Metacom. The war had been a violent Wampanoag uprising against the taking of their land by the English. Wampanoag and Algonquin warriors attacked throughout Plymouth Colony and killed many settlers. Although most of the violence was in 1675, tensions with indigenous Americans remained high in 1692, and colonists feared attacks. Adding to these woes were an epidemic of smallpox and, in Massachusetts, a bitter class resentment between impoverished Salem Village (today's Danvers) and the more affluent Salem Town (which is Salem today). In addition, the British crown was consolidating a number of Massachusetts colonies, not all of them Puritan, into one; the Puritans who had founded the Massachusetts Bay Colony were losing power and felt that their religious freedom, for which they had settled in America in the first place, was being diminished.

In January 1692, in Salem Village, nine-year-old Elizabeth Parris and eleven-year-old Abigail Williams, daughter and niece of Samuel Parris, the Salem Village minister, were possessed by violent seizures. Modern scientists suspect they were victims of a fungus, the ergot fungus, which is found in grains, especially rye. Lyme disease and epilepsy cannot be ruled out. But the diagnosis of the village doctor, William Griggs, was that they had been bewitched.

The twitching girls satisfied village authorities by naming the witches who had entranced them. They selected the three most defenseless women in the village, women who had little possibility of fighting back.

BIG LIES

They were Tituba, a slave whom Parris had bought in Barbados; Sarah Good, a penniless vagrant; and Sarah Osborn, an impoverished elderly woman.

Only Tituba, who may have been a South American native sold into slavery in the Caribbean, confessed. In doing so she named numerous other women who had worked with her on behalf of the devil. There is evidence that Parris beat her into confessing, and later she recanted her confessions, though some of those she named were hanged anyway. Parris, furious when she retracted her confessions, sold her.

Panic spread among the accused and the accusers. Many confessed. Among the accused was Sarah Good's four-year-old daughter. It was also time for the poor of Salem Village to exact some vengeance on the well-to-do of Salem Town, so a number of prominent women were also accused.

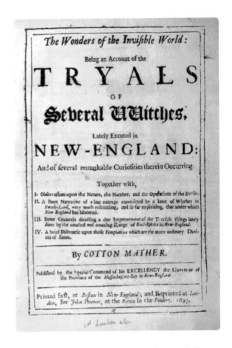

The Reverend Cotton Mather, minister of the Old North Church in Boston, wrote *Wonders of the Invisible World: Being an Account of the Tryals of Several Witches, Lately Executed in New-England* in 1692 to celebrate the Salem witch trials. After eleven of the accused had been executed, he wrote a letter to the presiding judge (whose appointment he had helped secure) congratulating him on "extinguishing of as wonderful a piece of devilism as has been seen in the world." As negative reactions to the executions built, Mather revised his account to minimize his own involvement, but he never disavowed his enthusiastic cheerleading of the trials.

The frenzy spread through the colony, and in May the governor ordered a tribunal. Two hundred people were accused, and twenty were hanged that summer, including six men who had refused to cooperate and even accused the accusers of being liars. Giles Corey, whose wife was one of the upper-class women accused, was laid prone in a field under a board on which more and more heavy stones were piled. This torture was designed to extract a confession, but he never confessed; after a few days of this, he died. His wife was hanged.

One accusation had its roots in a disagreement over a loan repayment. The real sin of Martha Carrier, one of several Andover women to be hanged, was being a member of a family that was believed to have introduced smallpox to the community. Seven accused women died in jail.

Deeply unpopular in Massachusetts, the tribunal was eventually shut down. In 1697 the Massachusetts General Court declared a day of fasting in remembrance of the victims.

The trials were ruled unlawful in retrospect, and in 1711, restitution was paid to the heirs of the victims.

The Salem witch trial was generally seen as a disgrace, and the reputations of those involved suffered. Nathaniel Hawthorne, author of the celebrated anti-Puritan novel *The Scarlet Letter*, changed the spelling of his surname out of shame that his great-great grandfather, John Hathorne, was one of the Salem judges.

But today the town of Salem uses its witch history as a tourist attraction. There is a "witch dungeon" with a live show, a tour of a pseudo witch village, a witch museum, and a coven of witches in a wax museum. There are similar attractions in the Basque village of Zugarramurdi, which has built a tourist trade, complete with souvenirs, on its checkered past as the scene of witch trials. Tourist promotions in both Salem and Zugarramurdi suggest that there really were witches there, which just shows how hard it is to kill a lie.

FROM RUSSIA WITH LOVE – PART 4:
BACK IN MAINE, **A WEEK LATER** . . .

DICK AND JANE ARE WATCHING
TELEVISION, AND TO THEIR SURPRISE,
EMILY LOVE COMES ON SCREEN.
SHE'S **SELLING CAR INSURANCE**.

TURN TO PEOPLE
YOU CAN **TRUST**!

. . . SHE SAYS TO THE CAMERA,
AND SHE DOES INDEED LOOK
LIKE **SOMEONE YOU CAN TRUST**,
JUST AS SHE DOES IN THE
PHOTO ON HER BLOG.

BUT AFTER WATCHING THE COMMERCIAL,
JANE REALIZES THAT **SOMETHING ISN'T RIGHT**.

DIDN'T **EMILY LOVE** SAY
THAT SHE'S A **HAIRDRESSER** IN HER
BLOG? WHAT'S SHE DOING ON TV
SELLING CAR INSURANCE?

DICK AGREES, SO HE **CALLS THE CAR
INSURANCE COMPANY** AND REACHES
A MAN NAMED **BOB WHITE**.

"I'M SORRY," SAYS MR. WHITE. "I DON'T KNOW WHO EMILY LOVE IS. *SOUNDS LIKE A PHONY NAME* TO ME."

SO DICK *CALLS THE ADVERTISING AGENCY* THAT CREATED THE CAR INSURANCE COMMERCIAL. HE HAS DIFFICULTY REACHING A REAL PERSON, *BUT HE IS DETERMINED*.

"*BRENDA HOPS* IS THE TALENT FOR THE AD YOU SAW," AN ASSISTANT NAMED *DOUG DEEP* FINALLY TELLS HIM. DEEP HAS A VERY DEEP VOICE.

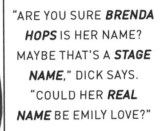

"ARE YOU SURE *BRENDA HOPS* IS HER NAME? MAYBE THAT'S A *STAGE NAME*," DICK SAYS. "COULD HER *REAL NAME* BE EMILY LOVE?"

DOUG DEEP LAUGHS. "WHY WOULD SOMEONE WHO ALREADY HAS A PERFECT STAGE NAME LIKE 'EMILY LOVE' CHANGE IT TO SOMETHING LIKE *BRENDA HOPS?*" BUT HE SAYS HE WILL PASS ALONG DICK'S QUESTION TO BRENDA.

A FEW HOURS LATER DICK RECEIVES A PHONE CALL. IT'S **BRENDA HOPS**.

"MY AGENT TOLD ME ABOUT YOUR CALL. **WHO IS EMILY LOVE?**" BRENDA ASKS DICK. "IS SHE USING **MY** AGENCY PHOTO ONLINE AND **LYING** ABOUT IT BY SAYING IT'S A PICTURE OF **HER**?"

DICK SUDDENLY REALIZES THAT **THERE IS NO EMILY LOVE**. SOMEONE HAD USED BRENDA HOPS'S AGENCY PHOTO TO CREATE A **FICTIONAL PERSON NAMED EMILY LOVE** IN ORDER TO **SPREAD DISINFORMATION ABOUT THE VACCINE** ONLINE. DICK TELLS THIS STORY ON SEVERAL SOCIAL MEDIA FORUMS . . .

. . . AND **THOUSANDS OF EMILY LOVE FOLLOWERS** ARE UPSET TO LEARN THAT **SHE DOESN'T REALLY EXIST.**

SOON EMILY LOVE IS **DELETED FROM ALL HER FORUMS** AS IF SHE WAS NEVER THERE.

DICK AND JANE **GET VACCINATED** AND . . .

. . . CELEBRATE WITH A BASKET OF **FRIED CLAMS**.

I LIKE THE BELLIES.

EVEN IF I COULDN'T TASTE THEM, I'D LIKE THEIR TEXTURE.

DICK'S A **LOYAL MAINER** TO THE END.

JANE MAKES A FACE.

YOU'RE WEIRD. BUT ANYWAY, I **FEEL A LOT SAFER** NOW.

DICK AGREES.

I DO FEEL SAFER FROM THE VIRUS, BUT I **DON'T FEEL SAFE** ABOUT A LOT OF OTHER THINGS. **WHO DO WE TRUST**, JANE? WE DON'T EVEN KNOW IF PEOPLE ARE **REAL** ANYMORE. **IS EVERYONE LYING**?

TO BE CONTINUED . . .

CHAPTER FIVE

A SNOWBALL IN FRANCE:

THE BLAME GAME

Is there any difference whatever between a lie and a conviction? All the world believes there is, but what does all the world not believe? An anti-Semite is certainly not made more decent by the fact that he lies on principle.
—Friedrich Nietzsche, nineteenth-century German philosopher

A lie is like a snowball: the longer you roll it, the bigger it becomes.
—Martin Luther (1483 – 1546)

Bigotry is the use of lies in the service of hatred.

Though its roots are difficult to understand, bigotry—prejudice against groups of people—has always been among us. Sometimes the motivation is obvious. If you want to exploit Black labor or rob wealth from Black countries, it is useful to claim that Black people are somehow unworthy of rights or wealth. If you want justification to steal a continent from those who were there before you, you need to show that they are unworthy.

There is a persistent myth that immigrants steal opportunities from citizens of the country to which they immigrate. This is almost always demonstrably untrue. It is a lie almost as old as immigration, but when the Trump campaign and administration once again repeated it, claiming that American citizens lose jobs and make lower wages because immigrants are willing to work for low pay, numerous researchers decided to look into this. Once again, the fallacy of these arguments was amply demonstrated. Brookings Institution senior fellow Vanda Felbab-Brown concluded in her 2017 essay "The Wall," "The impact of immigrant labor on the wages of native-born workers is low. Undocumented workers often work jobs that native-born workers are not willing to do." Other investigations show that because immigrants start businesses at a high rate, they create more jobs than they take.

All that can be said to justify bigotry against Jews, gypsies, or Muslims is that they are different from the Christian majority of the country in question, and people who are different cannot be trusted. Antisemitism, or bigotry against Jews, is one of the most persistent forms of irrational hatred in human history. It goes on and on; wherever and whenever there is bigotry, there is antisemitism. American racists are also anti-Semites.

Wherever haters hate, Jews are targets. Whenever there is a rise in bigotry, including this moment in history, there is a clear rise in antisemitism. Antisemitism is the model for bigotry.

According to this model, Jews are a sly people who secretly plot to take over the world. In some versions of this myth, known as "the secret Judah," they have already taken over and secretly run everything. The secret Judah lie goes back to the Middle Ages, though antisemitism is older than that. Such lies about Jews became more widespread and venomous in the late nineteenth century and have continued to this day.

What ignited the spreading of secret Judah conspiracies was that European Jews were becoming more assimilated. Originally hated for looking different, if they didn't *appear* different anymore, they were an even greater threat. If Jews looked and acted like members of the non-Jewish societies in which they lived, they could conceal their plans. The more "normal" they looked, the more they must be concealing. But Jews have always been an easy target because there are not many of them and (ironically, given antisemitic hysteria) they do not hold much power.

In Europe, antisemitism was part of the anti-Enlightenment. The French Revolution gave Jews, for the first time, full rights of citizenship. This made it possible for them to assimilate, and to a Jew hater that was a big mistake.

The French Revolution did not solidify in the government of France the way the American Revolution did in the US. France spent the nineteenth century in a bitter conflict between monarchists and republicans—between supporters of the old aristocracy and Catholic Church and the new egalitarian republic. As right-wing monarchists gathered force, this anti-Enlightenment movement became increasingly antisemitic and gained popularity by doing so.

French citizens whose lives had not been improved by the Enlightenment or the French Revolution felt powerless. They wondered who had taken their power away, though in truth they had never had any.

Politicians who told them that Jews were the problem gained their support, and the secret Judah lie emerged as a major political force.

A GREAT BRITISH LIAR

Religious differences have always been a rich field for liars, and religious persecution was never uniquely targeted at Jews. For a time, Catholics made a good target. Perhaps the greatest liar in British history was Titus Oates. In 1678, a time of great religious tension in England, Oates, a man of humble origin, launched a nation-shaking lie. He was already an experienced liar who had obtained a license as a preacher by faking a degree he never earned, but his new lie was by far his biggest. He wrote an elaborate document alleging a conspiracy in which the pope was plotting to take over England.

Oates claimed to have discovered that the pope was using monks of the Jesuit order to foment armed rebellion in Scotland and Ireland. Money had been collected and arms distributed. The king's assassination had been plotted in a London tavern. He was either to be poisoned by the queen's physician or shot with a silver bullet. Or there was a Jesuit agent with a foot-long dagger.

By the end of the nineteenth century the line was sharply drawn between the political left and right in France. In 1871, a group of leftist anti-church militants, the Commune, seized Paris and controlled the city for two months until they were brutally crushed by the French military, leaving enduring bitterness on both sides.

But the French military was not as successful against the Germans in the 1870 Franco-Prussian War. The Germans conquered and humiliated France and annexed territory from eastern France. How could Germany have defeated what the French had thought was the greatest military power on earth? This caused the downfall of France's latest attempt at a monarchy, the Second French Empire under Napoleon III, and a third attempt at a republic began. Out of power again, and still angry about the Commune's revolt, the anti-Enlightenment forces of the political right looked for a scapegoat to explain their failures and found one in the Jews. Obviously, the Jews had been secretly conspiring against France. They were behind the Commune, had secretly helped the Germans, and were sabotaging the economy besides.

This lie endured among right-wing elements in France as the best possible explanation for French failure. In 1894, a Jewish officer of the French general staff, 35-year-old Captain Alfred Dreyfus, was accused of passing information to the Germans. What became known as the Dreyfus Affair, a lie built on a forgery, shaped French history for the next half century.

Oates revealed these plots, based on absolutely no true evidence, to King Charles II, who doubted Oates's veracity. But, like many lies, this one caught on with no explanation.

A panic spread throughout England and led to the execution of fifteen innocent Catholics. Charles's successor, James II, tried Oates, convicted him of perjury, and sentenced him to be "whipped through the streets of London five days a year" for the remainder of his life. Oates was taken from his cell wearing a hat on which was written "Titus Oates, convicted upon full evidence of two horrid perjuries" and put into a pillory where passers-by pelted him with eggs. For days he was publicly stripped and beaten at various locations. The presiding judge at his trial, a man named Jeffreys, had helped to condemn innocent people on the basis of Oates's fabricated evidence. Now he was giving his former collaborator the harshest punishment possible. Some historians believe that the harshness of his sentence was from frustration that there was no death penalty for lying. Oates was eventually released during the reign of William and Mary, and he died in obscurity.

The Affair, as it came to be known, unfolded with more twists and turns than a good mystery novel.

Emile Zola published his "J'Accuse" open letter to the French president in January 13, 1898 issue of *L'Aurore*.

The evidence against Dreyfus was a letter, allegedly in the captain's handwriting, offering information to a German military attaché. On the strength of this fraudulent letter, Dreyfus was sentenced to life imprisonment. The decision was popular. At last a Jew had been caught conspiring with the enemy, confirming what "everyone" knew to be true. Dreyfus was sent to France's most infamous prison, the *bagne,* a penal colony on the steaming equatorial coast of French Guiana in South America.

In 1896, a new chief of the information division of the general staff, Colonel Picquart, became convinced that Dreyfus was innocent and that a Major Walsin-Esterhazy had been the one sending letters to the Germans. The handwriting in the evidentiary letter clearly matched Walsin-Esterhazy's penmanship and did not match Dreyfus's, but Picquart was told that Jews have studied handwriting for years to pull such tricks. Picquart was removed from his job and sent to a dangerous post in Tunisia. A closed-door trial found Walsin-Esterhazy innocent despite a mountain of damning evidence that Picquart had sent to the Dreyfus family's lawyers.

Dreyfus's innocence became a cause, and Émile Zola, one of the best-known French writers, published in 1898, in the newspaper *L'Aurore,* a long open letter to the

ALFRED DREYFUS'S PRISON CELL

Some years ago I visited Dreyfus's cell. It was not an easy thing to do. It is on an island so small that one shore is only a few minutes' walk from the other. No one had been there since Dreyfus left in 1899. He was imprisoned on the island alone, so there was no need for guards. Food was dropped off from time to time. The island is surrounded by a turbulent sea, and the coast is so jagged and rocky that it is impossible to land a boat. A military policeman agreed to take me in his Zodiac, an inflated raft with an outboard engine. He would come alongside the rocks, and I would roll out.

The officer seemed a kind and pleasant man, happy to help an inquiring writer. When he said he would be back in one hour, I joked, "Yeah, maybe that's what they told Dreyfus, too."

He smiled as he revved up his motor. "*Au revoir, Dreyfus deux,*" he said as he departed, and suddenly I realized that if he did not return, I could never get off the island. There is still an anti-Dreyfus, antisemitic element in French society, and this gendarme could be one of them. Maybe he didn't like this Jew paying respects to Dreyfus.

It was the longest hour of my life. There was only one building, the shack where Dreyfus was once chained. The roof was gone, and the iron bars on the window were rusted through. The wooden platform that served as a bed was still there. I tried to imagine the despair of this bourgeois Frenchman from a successful family marooned in the tropical heat for a lie he had no possibility of correcting.

There was no place else to go on the island, which had become a dense forest of palm trees. Coconuts are seeds, and when they fall to the ground, if undisturbed, they grow into palms. I kept looking at my watch. I had watercolors with me and killed time by painting a still life of the shack. I took my time. When I was done, either the gendarme would be there or I would start to panic. He arrived a tense three minutes late, smiling and pleasant, and helped me into his boat.

French president. In the letter, titled "J'accuse" ("I accuse"), Zola laid out the case for Dreyfus's innocence and listed the officials who were lying. Zola was immediately tried for libel and sentenced to a year in prison and a fine of 3,000 francs, but Dreyfus was pardoned by the president a year later. Zola received numerous death threats in the following years, and when he died from asphyxiation in his home in 1902, it was suspected that an anti-Dreyfus workman had stopped up his chimney.

The Affair rallied anti-Semites as well as Jews around the world. Celebrated Yiddish storyteller Sholom Aleichem (1859–1916) wrote a story about the impact of the Dreyfus case in Kasrilevke, a small, fictitious Jewish village, or shtetl, in Russia. "Paris, they tell me, boiled like the water in an overheated kettle. Newspapers wrote, generals shot themselves, Frenchmen ran about the streets like crazy people, throwing their hats in the air." The people in the shtetl, like most Jews around the world, embraced the persecuted Frenchman.

"The entire little village instantly took Dreyfus to heart, He became one of theirs, a Kasrilevker. Where ever there were two, Dreyfus was the third." This was probably true in most Jewish communities.

Theodor Herzl, an Austrian Jew sent to Paris by *Neue Freie Presse, a* leading Viennese newspaper, reported on the Dreyfus Affair. He was a secular Jew, part of what was called the Jewish Enlightenment, but his reporting on the antisemitic persecution of Dreyfus and on street demonstrators shouting "Death to Jews" started him thinking of the need for a Jewish homeland. He became the founder of the Zionist movement and imagined Israel as a German-speaking socialist state for Jews.

Dreyfus was finally acquitted of all charges in 1906, but antisemitic organizations continued to insist on his guilt and the existence of a broader Jewish conspiracy, and the divide between Dreyfusards and anti-Dreyfusards continued to define French politics.

Ironically, an affair that had started with Jews being accused of siding with the Germans ended up with antisemitic anti-Dreyfusards siding with the Germans.

After the Germans invaded and occupied France in 1940, the country was divided in two, with the northern half under Nazi rule in Paris and the southern half ruled by Henri-Philippe Pétain. The anti-Dreyfusard right rallied behind Pétain, a French hero of World War I who was credited with winning the pivotal Battle of Verdun in 1916. After the Germans installed him as the proxy ruler of southern France, he persecuted Jews, took away their properties and rights, jailed them, and deported those of foreign nationalities to Nazi death camps. It is often said that Pétain adopted the Germans' Nazi program, but he was not so much pro-German as anti-Dreyfus, even though by then the captain had been dead for years. Lies live longer than people. After the war, Pétain was convicted of treason. A major newspaper in the northern French city of Lille, *Voix du Nord,* covered the trial as a conflict between Dreyfusards and anti-Dreyfusards and wrote that a legal action could not settle this political conflict. "The country remains as divided as it was after the Dreyfus case," the paper wrote.

The idea that Jews were plotting to destroy France lived on, an example of what

Protestant reform leader **Martin Luther** had meant when he compared a lie to a snowball that got **ever bigger as it rolled on.**

Before social media and before radio, there were pamphlets—smaller and faster to read than books. A pamphlet titled *The Protocols of the Learned Elders of Zion* mysteriously appeared in Russia in 1903. It was so clumsily presented and so obviously a lie that it should have gone unnoticed. Instead, it has endured for more than a century.

The pamphlet claimed to be the stolen notes of a meeting of the secret central organization that controls all Jews. There never was such a meeting because there never was such a central organization of Jews, neither public nor secret. It is still unknown who concocted these fraudulent notes of a nonexistent meeting, but they are thought to have been written during the Dreyfus Affair, when similar theories of Jewish conspiracy were appearing across Europe. Some passages appear to have been plagiarized from Maurice Joly's 1864 satire against Napoleon III, *A Dialogue in Hell.* Ironically, Joly's book was a defense of an enlightened republic, the exact opposite of the intent of *The Protocols of the Learned Elders of Zion.*

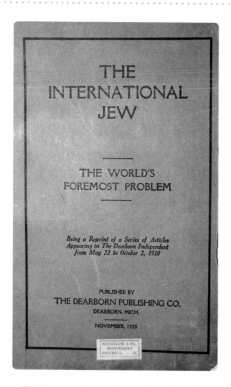

The International Jew: The World's Foremost Problem was a 1920 collection of articles that appeared in Henry Ford's newspaper, *The Dearborn Independent.* Ford hired a writer to frame his opinions for the articles. The book was translated into sixteen languages.

The pamphlet was an attempt to show that the Jews, a group of little power or influence, were in control. All the power centers that were running the world so ineptly—governments, politicians, military, the church—bore no responsibility for society's many ills because they had been hopelessly outmaneuvered by conniving Jews.

The text is a classic anti-Enlightenment tirade against science, egalitarianism, and the free press, with the added twist of blaming everything on Jews.

The *Protocols* was first used politically in 1905, when an uprising erupted across the Russian Empire and lasted two years, led by leftists, industrial workers, and peasants. More than 3,000 Russian troops were killed or wounded in fighting in which they killed 15,000 revolutionaries. Though the tsar regained control, the uprising was potent and widespread enough to deeply trouble the ruling establishment. How to explain this to their people? Obviously, it must have been a plot by the Jews, and the *Protocols* was the proof. The tsarist government had already explained that the Jews had caused their humiliating 1905 defeat in a war with Japan, the first modern defeat of a Western nation by an Asian one.

The *Protocols*, though poorly organized and awkwardly written, enjoyed tremendous international sales in the 1920s and 1930s. The great lesson is that a lie need not be plausible nor artfully presented. It need only offer a falsehood that suits enough people's needs, a story they want. Not only was it one of the most widely distributed publications in the world, it prompted the publication of some one thousand supporting books. Between 1920 and 1927, automobile manufacturer Henry Ford introduced Americans to the *Protocols,* translating them into English and running them in the weekly Michigan newspaper he founded in 1901, *The Dearborn Independent*. Also in Michigan, Father Charles Coughlin, a Catholic priest whose antisemitic radio broadcasts were extremely popular in 1930s America, referenced the *Protocols* as evidence of a Jewish conspiracy. Coughlin was a pioneer in talk

THAT *TITANIC* SINKING FEELING

The luxury liner *Titanic* hit an iceberg in the North Atlantic and sank in the night of April 15, 1912. More than 1,500 people died. It was tragic, but it was no mystery. Facts seldom slow down a good conspiracy theory, however, and one such theory is that the accident was no accident at all, but a deliberate insurance fraud. Another already-damaged ship, the *Olympic*, was deliberately sunk in the *Titanic*'s place for the insurance money. This does not explain the missing *Titanic* or the accounts of survivors or the discovery of the ship's remains on the seafloor in 1985, but so what?

There are many other theories. According to one, J.P. Morgan had the ship sunk to kill off competing millionaires Jacob Astor, Isidor Straus, and Benjamin Guggenheim, all of whom were on board. According to another, they were done in by the Rothschild banking house. The Rothschilds were Jewish, and theories about conspiring Jews were trendy.

radio, one of the first talking heads to understand that the new medium allowed him to spew lies with no one to contradict him.

Along with his translations, Ford ran a series of articles on how the

Apparently they still are, since QAnon, a leading purveyor of conspiracy theories today, has revived the theory that the Rothschilds sank the *Titanic*. Of course, two of the three supposed targets, Guggenheim and Straus, were also Jewish, but never mind that.

Jews were undermining American society and culture through various means including banking, labor unions, gambling, and jazz music. Published in book form, the articles sold a half-million copies in the US and were translated into sixteen languages. Hitler read the book in German and frequently quoted from it.

But Ford, facing a lawsuit, backed down, apologized for spreading what he admitted was a lie, and shut down his newspaper in 1927. Ford thought of himself as a leading Detroit citizen and was perplexed when a prominent rabbi refused his gift of an automobile.

A popular joke
among Detroit Jews was that a fortune teller told Ford he would

die on a Jewish holiday. "Which holiday?" the carmaker wanted to know. "Mr. Ford, any day that you die will be a Jewish holiday."

The *Protocols* continued to spread no matter how many times it was exposed and denounced, and it still appears in the Middle East and elsewhere in the world. It has recently been published in South America, Europe (Croatia), and Asia (Pakistan and Malaysia), and it is always at hand on the internet.

In Germany, lies were built on lies. After Pétain's triumph at Verdun in 1916 (really, more of a costly draw), the tide of World War I started to turn against Germany, but Kaiser Wilhelm decided that the German public should not know this. Instead, the German public was continually regaled with the triumphs of the German army, with the result that the country was completely unprepared when, in 1918, Germany surrendered and accepted humiliating terms, giving up territory and agreeing to pay huge war reparations to France that devastated the German economy. Germans wondered how this could have happened when they had so obviously been winning the war. Clearly they must have been betrayed, but by whom? Ah yes, it was the Jews who had stabbed them in the back. The Jews supposedly state in the *Protocols*, "It is indispensable for our purpose that wars, as far as possible, should not result in territorial gains." While we were winning, the Jews engineered our defeat.

The sign at the entrance of Auschwitz, the largest of the Nazi concentration camps, read *Arbeit macht frei*—Work makes one free. Six million Jews died in the Holocaust.

Amidst the wreckage and devastation caused on all sides by the pointless war, it became popular to say that Jews caused wars to beat countries into submission. Defeated Germans were not the only ones to make this claim. In 1918, before Germany's surrender, a British right-wing journal, *The Imperialist,* claimed to have uncovered a plot in which the British ruling family was conspiring with Jews to hand over Britain to the Germans. Even after victory, anti-Dreyfusards in France continued to claim that the wasteful, brutal war had been a Jewish plot that caused more than 20 million deaths. Louis-Ferdinand Céline, a well-known avant-garde French writer, declared in the 1930s that all European wars since 843 AD had been secretly caused by Jews.

Henry Ford also explained in his newspaper how the Jews had engineered World War I. Europeans had destroyed themselves for centuries in warfare pursued with reckless abandon; now they decided that it had all been done by Jews. This conspiracy theory was made to order for Adolf Hitler, and he took full advantage.

There is a famous line in the 1942 Michael Curtiz film *Casablanca*. When something goes wrong, the police captain's response is to say, "Round up the usual suspects." Often in this world, the usual suspects are Jews, Blacks, immigrants—anyone who can be "othered" because they are not part of a national majority. Has something gone wrong? Round up the usual suspects.

A LIE THAT CAME TRUE

Starting in 1914, a World War I battle zone known as the Western Front, from Belgium to France, produced hundreds of deaths almost every day. Since it was not clear exactly what they were fighting for, the British government worried about keeping their soldiers and the public motivated. It was considered essential to portray Germans as inhuman barbarians, and any lie that backed that up was a good lie. Writer Rudyard Kipling, an ardent British war backer, stated, "There are only two divisions in the world today, human beings and Germans."

It was an old trick. In 1588, to prepare for the invasion of the Spanish Armada, false stories were spread of the brutal Spaniards arriving with various implements of torture to use on the English if their attack succeeded.

At the beginning of the war, in August 1914, Germany invaded Belgium, which was supposed to be a neutral country, and that summer, in a new and brutal kind of warfare, killed 6,500 civilians in Belgium and northern France. The French interviewed refugees and spread unverified reports of atrocities, many of which were blatant lies. A *London Times* correspondent reported, "One man who I did not see told an official of the Catholic Society that he had seen with his own eyes German soldiery chop off the arms of a baby which clung to his mother's skirts." This suspiciously vague wording bears the hallmarks of an invented story. Who was the source, to whom did he report it, and where and when did the atrocity occur? The French produced a fraudulent photo of a baby without hands, and the article ran with drawings of German soldiers eating baby hands. Several inquiries during and after the war failed to produce any evidence that such a thing ever happened.

In 1915, as the war raged, a British commission led by a respected official, Viscount James Bryce, published the results of their investigation of

German atrocities. The commission cited many atrocities with almost no evidence, some of the wildest of which were alleged to have been committed against women and children. Amputations of children's hands and rapes and murders of women were claimed to be common practices. "We find many well-established cases of the slaughter (often accompanied by mutilation) of whole families, including not infrequently that of quite small children." No families, children, or locations were named. After the war, when the public began to question the truthfulness of the Bryce report, no basis could be found for any of these "well-established cases."

One of the most widely accepted lies was started by the *London Times*, which in April 1917 reported, "One of the United States consuls, on leaving Germany in February, stated in Switzerland that the Germans were distilling glycerine from the bodies of their dead." Glycerine, or glycerin, is a component of dynamite and blasting caps.

This is a classic example of an easily exposed lie. The tip-off is the vagueness. Who was this US consul? Where in Germany was this rendering of bodies happening? Where in Switzerland was the statement made? Where was the evidence? And yet it became commonly believed that the Germans were cooking down their war dead to make munitions. It showed what kind of horrible people they were—not people at all, really. By 1917 the British had spread many such lies about the Germans. The story of the German corpse factory lived on until it was debunked in 1925 and a British officer admitted having fabricated it.

The great tragedy was that in World War II the Germans really did abuse women and children, murder millions of civilians, make lamp shades and soap from humans, conduct horrifying medical experiments, and commit many other atrocities, but there was a reluctance to report on this for fear of sounding as questionable as the Bryce Report.

CHAPTER SIX

SOVIET MATHEMATICS: 2 + 2 = 5

Freedom is the freedom to say two plus two makes four.
—George Orwell, *1984*

In George Orwell's classic dystopian novel *1984*, an authoritarian regime keeps forcing people to say two plus two makes five. In time everyone is so used to hearing this that it becomes "as good as true." The idea of turning simple math to the service of lies was not invented by Orwell for his 1949 novel, however. Russian novelist Fyodor Dostoevsky, in his 1864 novella about an alienated man, *Notes from Underground,* writes about the seduction of lies, "I agree that two times two makes four is an excellent thing; but if we are dispensing praise, then two times two makes five is sometimes a most charming little thing as well."

Vladimir Lenin in 1919.

The rule of Joseph Stalin was marked by constant lies claiming the success of failed economic programs. His first "five-year plan" of 1928 was a massive failure by 1930, but he claimed it was a success, ahead of schedule after two years. In 1932 he claimed that the goals of the five-year plan had been completed after just four years. The slogan he drilled into the general population was that $2 + 2 = 5$.

It is often pointed out that Vladimir Lenin, one of the founders of the Soviet Union, said, "A lie told often enough becomes the truth." There is no record of him saying this exact thing, and it is possible that he never did, but it has been repeated so often that it is widely accepted as one of Lenin's most famous statements—thus, ironically, the statement proves itself. This quote is also sometimes attributed to Nazi propagandist Joseph Goebbels, but there is no record of him saying it either, though he certainly did practice it.

The reference to bogus math as a metaphor for lying has a long history. In Peoria, Illinois, on October 16, 1854, Abraham Lincoln said of Senator Stephen Douglas, "If a man will stand up and assert, and repeat and reassert, that two and two do not make four, I know nothing in the power of argument that can stop him."

If enough lies are told people become numb and stop searching for the truth.

Though all countries have a history of lying, the history of lying in Russia is particularly rich. The tsars with their conspiracy theories were notable liars. Soviet leaders continued to lie, and since the fall of the Soviet Union in 1991 the tradition has been maintained. Current Russian president Vladimir Putin—trained in mendacity as a Soviet intelligence agent—stands out for his lies, misdeeds, and denials.

But perhaps there has never been a more proficient Russian liar than Joseph Stalin, who consolidated his dictatorship over the Soviet Union by 1927 and ruled with an iron fist until his death in 1953. Millions died under Stalin's rule. He was skilled at accusing his political enemies of his own crimes and mistakes. He managed to appear flawless while his enemies were discredited and often killed, and then their murders were denied.

One of the standard techniques of a **lying government** is to attempt to rewrite history, to say things happened that didn't or **didn't happen that did.** Stalin literally rewrote history.

In 1928, while consolidating power, he released a new official history of the Russian Communist Party that remained the official version even after his death. In this version he played a more pivotal role than he had in the real world. Party leaders he didn't like, no matter how important, were not in this history.

For example, the new Soviet history included no one named Leon Trotsky. Trotsky had been at the right hand of Lenin, one of the key revolutionaries who played a central role in creating the Soviet Union. Most famously he created the Red Army, which defeated tsarist adversaries, secured the revolution, and went on to be an icon of Soviet power. He was Lenin's logical successor, but, partly because Trotsky was Jewish, Stalin was able to outmaneuver him and take the reins of power. Stalin then exiled Trotsky and expunged his name from Soviet history. All photographs of Trotsky disappeared. In exile he continued to write critically of Stalin until, in 1940, Stalin had him murdered in Mexico. Communist movements outside the Soviet Union that rejected Stalin's leadership continued to call themselves Trotskyites, but even today Trotsky is little known in Russia or other communist countries under Russian influence. Cubans, for example, are unfamiliar with the name, although his assassin, Ramon Mercader, lived out his days quietly in Cuba.

Leon Trotsky in 1924, at age 45.

One of Stalin's greatest lies was the cover-up of his failed farming cooperatives, his so-called five-year plans. An important component of the communist economic program was to eliminate private farms and have them taken over by government-run cooperatives. The plan didn't work, and millions starved to death in Ukraine between 1928 and 1933. It was part of Communist lore how Lenin had garnered attention during the 1891–92 famine in Russia's Volga River region by claiming that it showed the incompetence of the tsarist regime, and now the Communists could not be seen making the same mistake.

There were many reliable eyewitnesses to what Ukrainians call the Great Famine or the Holodomor, which was caused by Stalin's punishing policies (including confiscation of food from homes) as well as the failure of the farming collectives. But Stalin believed that a campaign of denial and fake facts could create enough confusion that his disaster would be hidden from the world.

Respected French leader Édouard Herriot arranged a fact-finding mission to Ukraine. On the day before his arrival, starting at two in the morning, peasants were made to clean the streets and decorate the houses. Food distribution centers were closed so there would be no long lines of desperate people waiting for food. Shop windows were filled with food, but the locals were not allowed to buy it or even to press too close to the windows. The most pitiable-looking people—homeless children and beggars on the street—simply disappeared. The hotel where Herriot was to stay was completely refurnished, and its staff were given smart-looking new uniforms.

The ruse worked, but stories of starvation continued to leak to the West. The Soviets acknowledged that there was some hunger and some malnutrition. They took pains to appear reasonable. *New York Times* correspondent Walter Duranty, who had received a Pulitzer Prize for his reporting on the Soviet Union and had even met with Stalin, reported, "there is no famine or starvation, nor is there likely to be." Senior journalists such as Malcolm Muggeridge and Joseph Alsop insisted that Duranty's stories were false, and they continued to report on the huge unfolding tragedy. Muggeridge characterized Duranty as "the greatest liar of any journalist I have met in fifty years of journalism."

Though there was solid reporting of many millions starving to death, Stalin succeeded in sowing enough doubt that the reports did not always receive broad acceptance. Doubt and confusion are the marks of a good liar.

Stalin went on to use the same technique to hide other crimes, such as his "show trials" in 1936–38, in which he eliminated political adversaries with fake accusations and rigged trials. Duranty defended the show trials, too. In 1990 the Pulitzer Board considered revoking Duranty's prize, though he had died in 1957, but they decided that despite much dubious work, the articles on life in the Soviet Union for which he had won the award were valid.

The Germans later adopted Stalin's Ukraine approach to cover up their concentration camps. In June 1944 the Red Cross was allowed to visit the Theresienstadt concentration camp, a holding spot for shipping Jews to death camps.

In preparation for the visit, gardens were planted and houses were painted and decorated.

Social events were staged for the Red Cross representatives. After they left, the camp returned to the business of genocide.

By the end of the war, 33,000 people had died in Theresienstadt, which had a crematorium that could burn 200 bodies a day. With no international effort to stop the carnage, 90,000 people were shipped from there to their deaths in other camps.

There are numerous other examples in various countries of doctoring up blighted areas for public events or invited dignitaries. There have been so many artificially constructed towns or settings in history that there is a name for them, Potemkin villages. Not all of them have been created by Stalinists and Nazis. American cities have had paper constructions and lighting to make slums look better for sporting events. In 1992 Mayor Ed Koch dressed up the Bronx by putting decals, venetian blinds, and potted plants in the windows of abandoned buildings. In Tibet, the Chinese have built model villages that remain uninhabited except when nomadic Yak herdsmen are forced to move in as a display to foreigners of the progress China is making there. Enron, a Houston energy company, constructed a fake trading floor on the sixth floor of its headquarters to convince visiting Wall Street analysts that nonexistent financial activities were taking place. In 2001, the company's activities were exposed as an elaborate fraud.

But the original Potemkin village may itself have been a lie. Gregory Potemkin, a government minister and lover to eighteenth-century Russian Empress Catherine II, allegedly built prosperous fake villages to make the countryside appear more affluent for the empress's 1787 boat tour of Crimea. There were not only fake buildings, but a single animal was moved around to look like a herd, or a small herd was moved from fake town to fake town as the empress's boat passed by. As it turned out, however, these stories were invented by a Finnish diplomat and a Saxon one. Turkey had recently lost the Crimea to Russia, and the Finns and Saxons wanted the Turks to think the Russians were weak and failing so they would attempt to take the Crimea back. The Potemkin villages never existed, but, like many successful lies, the story lived on.

ADJUSTING MEMORY

The word "genocide" is a combination of the Greek word for race and the Latin for kill. The word was invented in 1944 in a book by a Polish Jew, Raphael Lemkin, *Axis Rule in Occupied Europe*. Lemkin defined genocide as "a coordinated strategy to destroy a group of people, a process that could be accomplished through total annihilation as well as strategies that eliminate key elements of the group's basic existence."

A recent US government study estimated that between 1956 and 2016, forty-three incidents of genocide killed 50 million people.

Lemkin was writing about Nazi policies to kill off Jews, Poles, and other ethnic groups in Europe, but he first became interested in the crime of genocide as a student learning of the Turkish massacre of Armenians in Anatolia during and following World War I.

Armenians were a Christian people in the Muslim Ottoman Turkish Empire. Though persecuted in numerous ways, they managed to prosper, but between 1894 and 1896 hundreds of thousands were slaughtered in their villages by Turkish military forces in response to Armenian demands for fair treatment. Years later, during World War I, the Ottoman government became obsessed with the idea that Armenians hoped the Allies would defeat the Turks and grant them independence.

On April 24, 1915, the Turkish genocide of Armenians began with the execution of several hundred leading intellectuals. Others were force-marched naked in the Mesopotamian desert until they died of exposure. Death squads ran through the countryside, drowning, crucifying, or burning Armenians alive. Of an estimated two million Armenians in Turkey, only 388,000 remained alive by 1922.

Turkish governments, through many changes, have consistently lied about the Armenian massacre. Turkey continues to claim that there was no massacre of Armenians, that they were simply killed as enemy combatants—though in fact they were civilians.

Genocide denial is not unusual. American history until recently seldom discussed the genocidal policies toward Native Americans. The Japanese deny the atrocities their military committed in Asia in the 1930s, including the butchering of 200,000 men and the rape of 20,000 women in Nanking, China, in 1937. The Japanese have said they were trying to free Asia from Western colonialism. The Belgians denied the brutal slaughter of half the population of the Congo, ten million Congolese, between 1885 and 1908, in forced labor for rubber production. In 1919 a Belgian government commission finally reported the truth.

Memory adjustment is a standard tactic of authoritarian governments. In China, no discussion is allowed of the government massacre of what foreign diplomats and journalists estimate were hundreds or even thousands of pro-democracy protesters on June 4, 1989, in Beijing's Tiananmen Square. On the twentieth anniversary of the massacre, journalists were prohibited from entering the historic square in the center of the capital, and access to social media and foreign news sites was blocked.

The Chinese government censors the internet by banning key words. According to a 2019 study from the University of Toronto and the University of Hong Kong, more than 3,200 words cause the deletion of a post because it could possibly be discussing Tiananmen Square. The Chinese people can learn of a range of wild theories on the internet, but they will find nothing about the Tiananmen Square massacre.

As of 2021, Brazil's President Jair Bolsonaro was attempting to reestablish a Brazilian dictatorship by denying that there ever was one. In 2019 he tried to celebrate the 1964 coup d'état that brought in the bloodiest dictatorship in Brazilian history, murdering hundreds, often in so-called "accidents," while imprisoning and torturing thousands. Bolsonaro denied this history and claimed that the dictatorship had ushered in democracy. To confuse dictatorship and democracy, to say democracy doesn't work while at the same time claiming to be upholding it, is a favorite trick of dictators—"to believe that democracy was impossible and that the Party was the guardian of Democracy," as George Orwell put it in 1984. Bolsonaro said that Brazilians don't know what democracy is. He hoped to redefine it by lying about the past.

The Turkish government insists on its version of the 1915 genocide and tries to control the discussion by making it a priority in foreign relations. It is deemed necessary to accept the Turkish lie for other nations to have friendly relations with Turkey. As a Muslim nation at the gateway to the Middle East, Turkey is considered an extremely valuable ally, so they have succeeded in having their lie accepted.

A century later, however, the wall is beginning to crumble. The United Nations recognized the genocide in 1985, as did Pope Francis in 2015. A 2015 poll of young people in sixteen countries found that 77 percent of respondents of ages 16 to 29 believed that a Turkish genocide of Armenians took place. (Only 33 percent of the young respondents in Turkey agreed.) Thirty-two countries now recognize the Armenian genocide, although the recognition did not come in most of these countries until the twenty-first century.

The New York Times first used the phrase "Armenian genocide" in 2004. In 2019 the US House of Representatives recognized the Armenian genocide and the Senate unanimously approved, but President Donald Trump refused to support the measure. Liars generally like a good lie. In 2021, when President Biden officially recognized the Turkish massacre of Armenians as genocide, the Turkish government characterized his decision as "a true misfortune for Turkey–US relations." Every now and then, though not very often, truth takes center stage in world affairs, even if it is a century late.

◇◇

In the twenty-first century, Ukraine, by now an independent democracy and no longer "the Ukraine," a territory of the Soviet Union, was again victimized by a Russian dictator's big lies. In 2022—having invaded and annexed the Crimean Peninsula of Ukraine eight years before—Vladimir Putin launched a general invasion of Ukraine, justifying it with a complete fiction.

Stalin's defeat of the Nazis in World War II remains the single greatest legend of Russian history. It has kept Stalin in high regard among some Russians even though he was a mass murderer. There is little discussion of the millions of Soviet soldiers who died needlessly because of the incompetence of Stalin's generals. Eighty years later, Putin tried to lie his way into this mythology by claiming that he was attacking Ukraine because it was controlled by Nazis. The Mother Country, he told Russians, was once again battling Nazism. In fact, Ukraine was a democracy led by a popularly elected president, Volodymyr Zelenskyy, who was not only Jewish but whose grandfather had fought in the Red Army against the Nazis. Putin's claims were prominently and repeatedly shared on social media.

By early March, with the invasion dragging on and costing thousands of lives, Putin lost confidence in his ability to control the narrative. He started closing down social media and threatened punishment for anyone challenging his version of events. The Russian parliament, under Putin's control, decreed a prison sentence of up to fifteen years for any journalist reporting so-called fake news, which included using the words "war" or "invasion" to describe what was, in fact, an invasion and a war of aggression.

CHAPTER SEVEN

The TRUTH about AMERICAN TRUTH

The first casualty when war comes is truth.
—California Senator Hiram Johnson, opponent
of US entry into World War I, 1917

On August 6, 1945, an American B-29 bomber dropped an atomic bomb on the Japanese city of Hiroshima.

Three days later, on August 9, a second B-29 dropped an atomic bomb on the Japanese city of Nagasaki. These were the first and so far the only nuclear weapons to have been used in war, and understandably, the US government was hesitant to discuss this.

America lied from the start, insisting on secrecy and never admitting that it was developing a nuclear weapon. When a bomb was tested on July 16, 1945, the government explained that the huge explosion in the New Mexican desert, powerful enough to melt sand into glass, was "a harmless accident in a remote ammunition dump." The press and public didn't question the lie.

Even when the bomb was dropped on Hiroshima, the US government obscured its true nature. President Harry Truman said that day, "It is a harnessing of the basic power of the universe. The force from which the sun draws its power has been loosed against those who have brought war to the Far East."

An enduring part of the mythology is that the two bombings were a legitimate retaliation for the Japanese starting the war with an attack on Pearl Harbor. But Pearl Harbor was a military base attacked with conventional weapons. This was a nuclear bombing of two civilian targets, satisfying the international definition of a war crime. The US tried to claim that the Japanese targets were military, but military activity was not a priority in the choice of targets. The planners wanted the bombings to be "sufficiently spectacular." There was a base in Hiroshima, and 20,000 soldiers were killed in the blast, but so were between 70,000 and 126,000 civilians. Nagasaki had an even smaller military presence; of the 39,000 to 80,000 people killed, only about 150 were military. When the possibility of a third bomb was raised, Secretary of Commerce Henry Wallace said that Truman did not want more killing of "all those kids." The planners did understand that their victims were civilians.

The world's first nuclear explosion was this one in the desert of New Mexico, July 16, 1945, during the Manhattan Project.

Another enduring myth is that the attacks were carried out to force a Japanese surrender and avoid a costly and deadly invasion of the home island. But the Japanese military was finished. The Soviet Union's invasion of Japanese-controlled Manchuria just after midnight on August 9—hours before the bombing of Nagasaki— opened a new front against Japan and was one more confirmation to Japanese Prime Minister Hideki Tojo and his military command of their imminent defeat. Their fuel supplies had been destroyed, and they could no longer operate. It is true that there was disagreement on the terms of surrender, but they were ready to give up. Allied forces had known of the planned Soviet invasion since the Yalta Conference earlier that year, but the US military was ordered to drop the second bomb when ready. The bombing of Nagasaki was not contingent on whether the Japanese surrendered after Hiroshima.

After the surrender, the US military under General Douglas MacArthur took control of Japan and imposed strict censorship on the Western press, not even allowing correspondents into southern Japan. Japanese correspondents were strictly forbidden to mention anything about radiation in Hiroshima or Nagasaki. Books, films, and even letters leaving the country were censored. It was also strictly forbidden to mention anything about censorship.

On September 3, almost a month after the bombings, the first Western correspondent to make it into Hiroshima was Wilfred Burchett of the *London Daily Express.* With subterfuge and Morse code he was able to get his story back to London. His report was the first to describe a lingering deadly illness, radiation poisoning, that was painfully killing survivors. "In Hiroshima," he wrote, "thirty days after the first atom bomb destroyed the city and shook the world, people are still dying, mysteriously and horribly, people who were uninjured by the cataclysm—from an unknown something which I can only describe as the atomic plague."

Burchett had reported exactly what the US government did not want revealed, and the reaction was swift. American authorities asserted that there was no such thing as radiation sickness and accused Burchett of "falling victim to Japanese propaganda." In New Mexico, where the bomb was built in the Manhattan Project, the officer in charge, Major-General Leslie R. Groves, declared, "This talk about radioactivity is so much nonsense."

Would the US Army lie about a thing like this? There was healthy skepticism among journalists, a group of whom were invited to visit the test site in New Mexico.

They had to wear special shields over their shoes to keep **radioactive earth** from sticking, and they were followed by men with Geiger counters measuring their radioactivity. They were warned not to carry away any souvenirs. The reporters did not feel reassured.

Japanese scientists who studied the impact of the bombs were forced to turn their research over to the Americans. The US seized medical records and autopsy specimens. Confiscated blood samples and tissue biopsies were shipped to the US, and Major-General Groves continued his denials, telling *The New York Times* that if anyone died of radiation, "the number was very small," and reassuring the Senate that it was "a very pleasant way to die."

Survivors continued to suffer radiation illnesses and death. Their suffering has been documented despite their medical records being confiscated by US authorities for the next twenty-five years.

After the war, Truman met with J. Robert Oppenheimer, the scientist who had developed the bombs. Oppenheimer told the president that scientists had blood on their hands and had sinned. Truman left instructions after the meeting that he never wanted to see Oppenheimer again.

SITTING BULL'S PERSPECTIVE

The standard US tool for dealing with Native Americans was to force them into treaties designed to turn traditional hunters into farmers. If the treaty later proved inconvenient for the expansive ambitions of European Americans, if they wanted that land to build or mine, the treaty would be ignored. The entire legal process offered to Native Americans was a sham. Even treaties backed by Supreme Court decisions were ignored. The 1868 Fort Laramie Treaty granting the Black Hills territory of South Dakota to the Sioux was a typical example. When gold was discovered in the Black Hills, the federal government simply ignored the treaty and started forcibly removing the Sioux from their treaty land. Two leaders, Sitting Bull and Crazy Horse, united the Plains tribes to fight the US Army and achieved a famous victory against George Armstrong Custer on the banks of the Little Big Horn River.

Custer's widow, Elizabeth Bacon Custer, spent the rest of her life publishing lies and half-truths to improve the image of her arrogant, disastrous husband.

But the US Army could call in more soldiers and more firearms, while the systematic slaughter of the great buffalo herds was making traditional life impossible. Forced removal of the Sioux from their lands continued, and Sitting Bull and his people fled to Canada. Sitting Bull summed up the entire history when he told a Canadian government commissioner, "There is no use talking to these Americans. They are all liars. You cannot believe anything they say."

In 1962 Paul Ekman, a psychologist who had earned recognition for his research on the relationship of emotions to facial expressions, observed a tense negotiation between President John F. Kennedy and Soviet Foreign Minister Andrei Gromyko. He concluded with admiration that both men were "natural liars, inventive and clever in fabricating; smooth talkers, with a convincing manner."

On July 20, 1969, when the Americans landed on the moon, it was already accepted that the US government sometimes lies. Enough victims of Hiroshima and Nagasaki came forward in the 1950s and 1960s to make clear that the US had been untruthful about radiation poisoning. In 1960, NASA lied for Eisenhower when a spy plane was shot down over the Soviet Union, claiming that the U-2 piloted by Francis Gary Powers was a research plane doing meteorological studies.

The start of the American war in Vietnam was based on a lie. Vietnam had been divided into northern and southern portions, with South Vietnam backed by the US against the Communist North. Under the direction of the US, the South Vietnamese navy was attacking radar stations, bridges, and other strategic targets along the coast of North Vietnam.

President Lyndon Johnson signing the Gulf of Tonkin Resolution into law on August 10, 1964. The resolution giving Johnson broad war powers was passed by Congress after testimony by Secretary of Defense Robert McNamara in which he lied intentionally. Army Colonel H. R. McMaster wrote in his 1997 book *Dereliction of Duty* that Johnson and McNamara "deceived the American people and Congress . . . . They used a questionable report of a North Vietnamese attack on American naval vessels to justify the president's policy to the electorate and to defuse Republican senator and presidential candidate Barry Goldwater's charges that Lyndon Johnson was irresolute and 'soft' in the foreign policy arena."

On the night of July 30–31, 1964, as the South Vietnamese attacked military targets in North Vietnam, the US destroyer *Maddox*, on patrol in the Gulf of Tonkin, was approached by North Vietnamese torpedo boats pursuing South Vietnamese attackers. The *Maddox* fired warning shots, but the torpedo boats continued and returned fire. The *Maddox* called in air support from a nearby aircraft carrier, and a North Vietnamese boat was seriously damaged. The *Maddox* was unharmed.

A second destroyer, *Turner Joy*, was sent to assist, and on the night of August 4 they insisted they were being attacked. A plane sent to investigate reported no boats attacking, and hours later the captain of the *Maddox* sent a message stating, "Review of action makes many reported contacts and torpedoes fired appear doubtful. Freak weather effects on radar and overeager sonar men may have accounted for many reports.... Suggest complete evaluation before any further action taken."

There had been no attack on August 4, but President Lyndon Johnson took advantage of the confusion to insist that the US had been attacked, and he used this as a pretext to go to war with North Vietnam.

The *Pentagon Papers*, stolen secret documents published in 1971, revealed that the Johnson administration had known that the Gulf of Tonkin attack had not taken place. It was a lie. The papers also revealed that Presidents Kennedy, Johnson, and Nixon had all lied about activities in Vietnam. Though it seemed scandalous at the time, it is not surprising to any war historian. Most wars are built on lies.

The Spanish American War, Vietnam, and Iraq were all started with founding lies. Napoleon, as his troops spread through Europe, was a spectacular and constant liar.

There were few facts and little honest reporting from war correspondents in the Civil War. They were mostly propagandists for their side. Fictitious horror stories of the brutality of the other side were invented. It was reported that Southern women wore necklaces strung with the eyeballs of Yankee soldiers. Fictitious battles were reported. Casualties were underreported. Enemy generals were falsely reported dead.

A cartoon for the June 1898 issue of *Vim* magazine shows Joseph Pulitzer (left), publisher of the *New York World*, contending with William Randolph Hearst, publisher of the *New York Journal*, for ownership of the Spanish-American War. The rumors and propaganda printed in both newspapers helped goad America into war. Sensationalist newspaper reporting was dubbed "yellow journalism."

In February 1898, the US battleship *Maine* exploded while on patrol in Havana Harbor. The cause of the explosion, in which 260 American sailors died, has never been determined. It may have been accidental, as the Spanish government insisted. A 1976 Navy investigation claimed the explosion was caused by a coal bunker fire. But claiming without evidence that the Spanish had sunk the vessel made a good pretext for war. The popular battle cry was "Remember the *Maine*."

Propelled by

William Randolph Hearst's *New York Journal,* so many lies were issued about the war that the phrase "fake news" was born. One paper, *The St. Paul Globe,* even added to their front page the motto "No Fake War News."

This detail from a cartoon in an 1894 issue of *Puck* magazine shows that the term "fake news" was already in use and could be applied by a demagogue to any journalist who inconvenienced him.

The US pretended to fight the Spanish-American War in support of Cuban independence from Spain. But once the Spanish were driven out, the occupying Americans made clear that they simply wanted to replace the Spanish as colonial overlords. This lie is still at the root of US-Cuban conflict.

At the time of the moon landing,

the United States and the Soviet Union were in a tight race for space exploration. The Soviets had placed the first human-made object on the moon in 1959, and they could land ships on the moon and accomplish other feats as well as or better than the US. In the early 1960s it came to President Kennedy's attention that the one area where the US had an advantage was the possibility of landing men on the moon and bringing them home safely. This was because the US had developed lighter-weight equipment.

On July 20, 1969, Apollo 11 delivered lunar capsule *Eagle* to the moon, and two astronauts, Neil Armstrong and Edwin "Buzz" Aldrin, stepped out and walked on the lunar surface. They spent two and a half hours there, planting a flag, and then left. The event was recorded on slow-scan television tapes as well as still photographs. An estimated 530 million people around the world watched on their televisions. Between 1969 and 1972, six NASA missions put a total of twelve astronauts on the moon.

And yet, after the first landing was celebrated as a **great triumph,** some started to call it a lie and said **it had never happened.**

The idea that the landing had been faked was particularly popular in the 1970s but persists to this day.

NASA's motive (according to conspiracy theorists) was to claim they had beaten the Soviet Union in the so-called space race. It is interesting that the Russians, the would-be victims of the hoax, who love conspiracy theories, never signed on to this one. There was too much scientific evidence, and the Soviets had good space science. They launched their own lie instead, saying that the space race itself was a hoax and that Russia had never been competing. US astronauts who later visited Soviet space centers have refuted this.

From 1972 to 1974, the Watergate scandal

revealed one lie after another from the Nixon administration. In 1974

Jimmy Carter ran for president denouncing the lying of the US government and promising that he would not lie. In his memoirs he wrote, "I was deeply troubled by the lies our people had been told; our exclusion from the shaping of American political and military policy in Vietnam, Cambodia, Chile, and other countries; and other embarrassing activities of our government, such as the CIA's role in plotting murder and other crimes."

Carter tried to keep his promise—it is hard to find lies he told as president, though there may have been a few—but the Carter administration did not put an end to lying. In 1986, the Reagan administration was caught in a trifecta of mendacity, a lie on a lie on a lie. While the US was boycotting trade with Iran, Reagan's team offered the Iranians weapons in exchange for the release of American hostages in Lebanon. At the same time the arms deal would generate funds that could be secretly funneled to an armed group in Nicaragua called the Contras. Reagan compared the Contras to "the founding Fathers," but in fact they were an old oligarchy determined to reestablish the overthrown dictatorship and funded largely by trafficking cocaine. Congress had forbidden funding of the Contras.

Reagan originally denied everything, but a week later retracted his denial. Marine Colonel Oliver North was indicted for these illegal dealings. North called the crimes "covert operations," intelligence secrets, and said such operations "are at essence a lie."

There is always a debate between a national security interest and a lie. Recognizing that governments have the need and the right to keep secrets means accepting that governments sometimes lie.

Czech novelist Milan Kundera wrote, "Having a public, keeping a public in mind, means living in lies." But once lying becomes acceptable, it can be used to cover all sorts of sins and even crimes. Even if it was necessary to lie about developing the atomic bomb, was it necessary to lie after dropping it? In the Iran/Contra scandal, national security was used as an excuse to cover up illegal activity. North said he had top government approval for the operation and had assumed Reagan was behind it, but the activity was completely illegal. It involved no vital secrets that the country needed to protect. Although indicted, North made himself into a hero (for some) by claiming he

Lieutenant Colonel Oliver North testifying at the Iran-Contra hearings in 1987. North served as president of the National Rifle Association from September 2018 to April 2019.

had acted for the good of America. He was convicted of lying and conspiracy, but the convictions were overturned on appeal, and he became a conservative television host. *Washington Post* editor Ben Bradlee said, "He proved once again that a great actor can save even a lousy script." Fourteen people were charged in all, but Reagan wasn't one of them. Only one of those convicted served any jail time, a businessman who was convicted of underreporting his earnings from the scandal.

President George W. Bush invaded Iraq on the insistence that the Iraqi regime was building "weapons of mass destruction," nuclear and chemical weapons, and had to be stopped. This is an example of a lie with no legs at all. There was no evidence that the story was true; the only people who had seen what was happening in Iraq, international weapons inspectors, insisted that there was no sign of any weapons of mass destruction. But the Bush team pushed on against all facts.

The lie ruined careers. Secretary of State Colin Powell, a former general, played the loyal soldier and went to the United Nations insisting on his president's story without any evidence. "There can be no doubt," he told the United Nations, "that Saddam Hussein has biological weapons and the capability to rapidly produce more, many more." It was not true. Once Iraq was invaded, a government report said that the intelligence was "dead wrong." Powell later described the speech as "a blot" on his career. In his 2012 memoir, *It Worked for Me,* he wrote, "I am mad mostly at myself for not having smelled the problem. My instincts failed me."

Indeed, the instinct to smell out a lie is an important leadership skill.

Powell predicted, "The event will earn a prominent paragraph in my obituary." When he died in 2021, this proved correct. The blot ruined his career. He had often been mentioned as a possible candidate to be the first Black American president. Instead, he retired from politics.

Tony Blair was a young, charismatic British prime minister whose popularity had revived the waning British Labour Party. That was until 2002, when he announced that Iraq was building weapons of mass destruction and had to be stopped. British intelligence, he told his people, had concluded "that Iraq has chemical and biological weapons, that Saddam has continued to produce them, that he has existing and active military plans for the use of chemical and biological weapons, which could be activated within 45 minutes."

A 2004 investigation of the intelligence report on which he based these assertions concluded that it was "unreliable" and that Blair made the evidence appear far stronger than it was. Blair admitted being wrong but denied lying. Many, including Conservative leader Michael Howard but also politicians from other political parties, concluded that Blair had deliberately lied in making the intelligence sound more conclusive than it really was. Labour politicians called for his expulsion from the party, and some demanded that he be banned from political leadership. A 2016 report prepared by Sir John Chilcot concluded that Blair misled the public and did not accurately describe what his intelligence report had said. The intelligence had not made the assertions that Blair claimed.

His popularity and that of the Labour Party declined rapidly, and in 2007 he resigned from office. He never recovered from the scandal.

Iraq's arsenal of mass destruction was a lie with no future. Bush must have known that if he were able to take Iraq, he would be expected to produce the nonexistent weapons. But the lie served its purpose. He got his invasion, and his popularity surged, reaping the wartime president's usual bonus of support from American voters. Once the Iraqi government was overthrown, the US military inspected all of Saddam's facilities and found no sign of chemical or biological weapon production. "We don't know what has happened to them," Tony Blair said of the missing WMDs. Probably few in the Bush administration were surprised. Some lies are for history, but others are for short-term goals.

Colin Powell displays a model of a vial of anthrax while telling the United Nations on February 5, 2003, that Iraq possessed weapons of mass destruction.

Even without weapons to show, Bush tried to create the illusion of victory. In 2003, with Iraq on the edge of civil war, he stood on the deck of an aircraft carrier, dressed in military uniform, and declared victory. It didn't work. The US was engaged in war in Iraq for the next eight years.

According to the Pentagon, more than 4,300 American soldiers died in Iraq after Bush declared victory.

President Bush delivers his "Mission Accomplished" speech on the deck of the USS *Abraham Lincoln*, May 1, 2003.

According to Iraqi officials, 85,000 Iraqis were killed, many of them civilians. The US government estimate was lower, but documents leaked by Wikileaks in 2010 showed that the US was intentionally lying. Hundreds of thousands of US military field reports documented 66,061 civilian casualties out of 109,000 Iraqi deaths. This revelation led to the formation of a group called the Iraq Body Count project that claimed to document 112,017 to 122,428 civilian deaths between 2003 and 2013. Some journalists have called this an overcount, others an undercount. It seems unlikely that the truth will ever be known, but it does seem that the Bush administration attempted to undercount. In lying about casualties, Bush was following a long-standing coverup.

Modern war
is waged against civilians. Starting with World War II, almost every war has killed more civilians than combatants.

But lying does not always come with a price. Somehow Bush survived the exposure of his costly lie and was elected to a second term, though just barely.

By the time Donald Trump came to office in 2017, compounding lie after lie, it seemed there was no penalty for presidential lying. The only president to be impeached for lying was Bill Clinton, who had precipitated no war and no deaths but had lied about a sexual encounter. This, apparently, was the one impeachable lie. He was impeached by the US House of Representatives but was not convicted in the Senate because few thought his lie rose to the level of a "high crime and misdemeanor" threatening the government and justifying his removal from office. In fact, the few who said it did were lying about the liar.

Could the US government be believed on anything?

Maybe the moon landing was a lie.

But in all these other scandals, witnesses had come forward to reveal the lies. None of the 400,000 technicians, scientists, engineers, machinists, and astronauts has ever supported the theory that the moon landing was a hoax. Such witnesses are essential to exposing a lie.

Like so many conspiracy theories this one has depended on ignoring science.

The theories are based on the look of the tapes and photos, which, in truth, do appear a little fake. That is because no one had ever shot footage on the moon before, and the images were unsophisticated and not what we expected. The big clue is that in photos the American flag is flapping in the wind. Aha! There is no wind on the moon. But the flag is not flapping; it is sticking out straight because a rod was placed in it to make it visible to TV viewers.

Why are there no stars in the sky? They are there but can't be captured by a camera in the lunar daylight.

If the sun were the only source of light, objects in shadows would not be visible, so the shot must be the product of Hollywood lighting techniques. Actually, the opposite is true. The lighting on the moon is different from what we are used to in that light reflected from the ground plays a greater role. If Hollywood had lit the scene, it probably would look more like what we are used to. Outer space as depicted in Stanley Kubrick's 1968 hit movie *2001: A Space Odyssey* looked more "real" to the public.

Astronaut Buzz Aldrin on the moon's surface on July 20, 1969, in a photo taken by fellow astronaut Neil Armstrong.

Kubrick had used scientists and artists to create the effects, and some people decided that Kubrick must have worked on the fake landing as well. But the moon landing did not look as real as the film.

> In the world we now live in, **it is sometimes a struggle to** realize that life is more real **than the movies. Many prefer the movies.**

Much science came from the six moonwalks of the Apollo missions. Anyone can acquire a laser and a telescope and prove that the Apollo 11 landing was real by bouncing laser beams off three retroflectors, devices designed to bounce radiation, usually in the form of a light beam, back to its source. The Apollo 11, 14, and 15 crews placed these on the moon. Most people (me included) do not know how to accomplish this relatively simple technological feat, but anyone troubled by the veracity of the moon landing can learn how to do it.

In 2009, NASA's Lunar Reconnaissance Orbiter started sending high-resolution photos of the Apollo landing sites. The photos show the rocket stages left behind by all the missions, including Apollo 11, as well as tracks and footprints of the astronauts.

But despite all evidence, according to pollsters, 6 percent of Americans still believe the landing was faked. It is said that Buzz Aldrin once punched someone for saying the flight was faked, but this story may also be false.

No mountain of evidence can convince everyone that a lie is a lie. For some people, just wanting it to be a hoax is enough.

CHAPTER EIGHT

BIG DICTATORS and BIG LIES

The central belief of every moron is that he is the victim of a mysterious conspiracy against his common rights and true desserts.

—H.L. Mencken, twentieth-century US journalist

George Orwell's dystopian vision of a totalitarian future is disturbingly accurate.

Many waited for the nightmare to come in 1984, but that year came and went without anything too cataclysmic. It was often pointed out that Ronald Reagan, a right-wing actor, absurdly had become president, but he served for eight years, certainly with consequences but nothing as drastic as Orwell had predicted. Orwell did not give it enough time, because in this century we seem to be inching closer to *1984*.

George Orwell's "big brother is watching you" warning expressed with binary code.

In Orwell's novel, the world is divided into three ruthless power centers who keep each other in check. One is run by the US, one by Russia, and one by China. Each is somewhat neutralized by its attempts to contain the other two. This may have seemed far-fetched in 1949 but describes reality today.

In Orwell's world, every room, every meeting place, every office, every conceivable space has at least one electronic screen. These screens are completely controlled by government. Orwell's fictional screens are now real. With a few exceptions, such as China, these screens are not government controlled and so are not completely a tool for totalitarianism, but they aren't completely a tool for freedom either.

As demand grows for policing of the internet, some kind of government regulation, a thorny question arises— how much government control is enough? It was, after all, the founding idea of the internet that it be a system for the free flow of ideas, where anyone's opinion counts and no one controls the dialogue. This is the biggest lie of our times.

The internet did not turn people into liars.

Every new idea in human communication has been seized on by liars. The invention of the alphabet and the written word, as Plato acknowledged, offered tremendous potential for liars. And think how much faster and farther lies could spread with the advent of the printing press.

Even a cookbook was used for propaganda. In seventeenth-century England there was a bitter civil war between forces led by Oliver Cromwell, who executed King Charles I and established a republic, and the royalists who reestablished the monarchy after Cromwell's natural death in 1658. The bitter divide continued. Cromwell's body was dug up and executed several times, though it is possible that none of these bodies were really Cromwell's. One head was kept in various places until the twentieth century.

In 1665 a cookbook was published, *The Court and Kitchen of Elizabeth, Commonly Called Joan Cromwell, the Wife of the Late Usurper*. The late usurper was Oliver Cromwell, and historians agree that the recipes do in fact come from the Cromwell kitchen. But the book most certainly was not written by Elizabeth, who avoided politics and never wrote anything. The cookbook is filled with diatribes against her late husband. This cookbook was yet another way to denounce Cromwell. A lying cookbook was a new way to lie.

Newspapers began at about this time and, like the internet more than three centuries later, presented tremendous opportunities for truth and lying. Pamphlets and single-page documents called broadsheets, such as the American Declaration of Independence, also began appearing.

The *New York Journal* front page of February 17, 1898. Joseph Pulitzer's *New York Journal* and William Randolph Hearst's *New York Post* competed through the 1890s with sensationalized, dramatized, salacious headlines and stories. Their use of exaggerated and manufactured claims to sell newspapers foreshadowed the click-bait headlines mass-produced by internet troll farms today. In 1898 the newspapers whipped up war fever with their "yellow journalism," a term derived from a popular *New York World* comic called "Hogan's Alley," which featured a yellow-dressed character named "the yellow kid."

Another huge upgrade in the potential for lying before the internet was radio. The technology was experimented with throughout the nineteenth century, although the word "radio" did not come into common use until the twentieth century, which ushered in its heyday. Radio was a tool for lying like nothing before it.

Somewhere between the explosion of printed propaganda and the development of radio, the nature of public lying changed.

In ancient times a public lie was a false statement designed to glean more support than a truth. But those seeking power started to realize that lying could alter reality, creating a different truth, an alternate truth. Twentieth-century German philosopher Hannah Arendt wrote, pre-internet, that "the ancients were satisfied with a passing victory of an argument at the expense of truth, whereas the moderns want a more lasting victory at the expense of reality."

To be a good liar no longer required skill at reasoning but, instead, boldness. It required mastery of what Orwell called "doublespeak," the ability to embrace contradictions while arguing passionately for both sides. For the Soviets, the Nazis, other dictators, supporters of US right-wing politicians, and many others—including most anti-Enlightenment enthusiasts—democracy became a favorite candidate for doublespeak. Democracy is a cheat and a fraud, but also, I am the defender of democracy.

Ultimately the goal is to create **so much confusion** that the public gives up trying to discern **truth from lies.**

In 2016, in an example of the positive use of social media, Garry Kasparov, Russian chess grandmaster turned political dissident, tweeted, "The point of modern propaganda isn't only to misinform or push an agenda. It is to exhaust your critical thinking, to annihilate truth."

A favorite ploy is to argue that the exposing of a lie proves that it is true. As Donald Trump's lies were exposed one after another by the established news media, he argued that if "fake news" said it was a lie, it must be true. In Hitler's version of truth, evidence that *The Protocols of the Elders of Zion* was a forgery only proved that the document was real. Otherwise, why would the Jews have gone to the trouble of refuting it?

"The party told you to reject the evidence of your eyes and ears," Orwell wrote in 1984.

The function of lies was no longer simply to deny a truth but to create a new one. As Spanish dictator Francisco Franco once put it, "We must be willing to defend, tenaciously and on all occasions, our truth." A successful liar creates a special truth that only supporters believe. The goal is not to convince opponents but to fuel supporters. Since this is what supporters want, why would they question it?

By the 1930s, liars had in radio a more powerful tool than had ever been known.

Today people talk of how quickly social media can spread hoaxes and panics, but this isn't new; radio had huge audiences. Franklin Roosevelt was one of the first to realize the power of radio. In 1933, Robert Trout, one of the first star radio news correspondents, announced, "The president wants to come into your home and sit at your fireside for a little fireside chat." Roosevelt did these radio chats regularly for nearly a decade, talking to the public in their homes about the Depression and World War II. When Trout first announced the chats on CBS radio, 41 percent of US cities had access to local radio stations. By Roosevelt's second term as president, about 90 percent of Americans had access to a radio.

Father Charles Coughlin in the late 1930s.

Radio, like all new media, could be used for good and bad. Father Coughlin, a Detroit-based Roman Catholic priest, had an estimated 30 million listeners around the country for his populist broadcasts in the 1930s that grew increasingly antisemitic and fascistic.

Orson Welles's Mercury Theatre set off a national panic in 1938 with a radio adaptation of H.G. Wells's fictitious *War of the Worlds.* The broadcast was so convincing that people around the US believed Martians were invading. The broadcast was not a political act, but it demonstrated the power of radio.

One of the greatest liars to master radio was Joseph Goebbels, Hitler's minister of propaganda. He is credited with making Hitler popular with the German people by using radio, although blaming radio for the German support of Hitler is like blaming social media for the rise of Donald Trump. Ultimately, the people themselves are responsible for their choices.

The Nazis garnered support after a humiliating military defeat that led to a crumbling economy. Still, Goebbels himself unabashedly credited radio for Hitler's rise.

"It would not have been possible for us to take power or to use it in the ways we have without the radio," he once said.

He did not just make up his own lies, he had a staff of nearly one thousand propagandists manufacturing lies, mostly for radio broadcast. He distributed radios to the public; having one of these official radios was a sign of being a good Nazi, not only because they were decorated with a swastika but because they were only capable of picking up Nazi party frequencies.

It was Goebbels who created the "Führer myth" that Hitler was a godlike genius leading Germany and the world to a bright future. Radio was used to promote nonsensical justifications for Nazi invasions. Hitler told Goebbels to simply invent these justifications. Hitler did not care if they were believable. Propaganda does not need to be credible. As Hitler said, "The victor will not be asked whether he told the truth."

All sides in World War II fought the war over the radio, and after the war the world had changed. In 1945, at the end of the war, Alexandre Koyré, a noted French philosopher and science historian, commented with a sense of urgency:

"Never has there been so much lying as in our day.

Never has lying been so shameless, so systematic, so unceasing." Koyré sounds like someone today complaining about social media, except that he was talking about radio.

To him, radio was just the latest perfection of mendacity. He wrote, "Lying has never had so massive, so total a character as it has today. The written and spoken word, the press, the radio, all technical progress is put to the service of the lie."

Koyré, among others, observed that the modern lie was different from old-fashioned lies. Because of mass media, "The distinctive feature of the modern lie is its mass output for mass consumption. And all production for the masses, especially all intellectual production, is bound to yield to lower standards." Lenin, Stalin, Hitler, and all the great modern liars acknowledge that the important trick is to be lowbrow. Goebbels said that "the rank and file are usually much more primitive than we imagine. Propaganda must therefore always be essentially simple and repetitious." This may be why New England–born, Yale-educated George W. Bush, from a patrician family, spoke in a folksy drawl. Donald Trump was often mocked for the misspellings and grammatical errors in his tweets, and this may have been truly Trump, but also he understood his audience.

Radio has proven remarkably durable. To the surprise of many, it prospered in an age of television. Radios, unlike televisions until much later, could be small, portable, and installed in cars. The first small transistor radios were marketed in 1954. The success of radios has meant a proliferation of good-quality news, but it has also given a platform to aspiring Father Coughlins.

"Talk radio"

became enormously popular and laid the groundwork for the **culture of lies on social media.**

Talk radio simply spews one person's opinions nonstop, without challenge. The opinions may be racist, sexist, and absurd lies, but it makes no difference, for there is no one to challenge. Callers are selected and can be ridiculed or cut off. The most successful of these new hosts, Rush Limbaugh, spewed hate and lies until his death in February 2021. Talk radio was primarily local before Limbaugh, but in 1988 he found a spot on WABC–AM and soon had five million listeners.

He said of an on-court brawl between two National Basketball Association teams that it was "hip-hop culture on parade." While acknowledging that his commentary would be tagged as racist, he went on to say, "Call it the TBA, the Thug Basketball Association, and stop calling them teams, call 'em gangs." He said, "Feminism was established so as to allow unattractive women access to the mainstream of society." He produced hundreds of these outrages and became enormously popular for it. Like all good public liars, he provided lies that his public wanted to hear. In his last year of life, he told us there was no threat from Covid-19. It was just made up by people who opposed Donald Trump. This resembled his denial of any connection between smoking and cancer. He said there was no risk from secondhand smoke,

Rush Limbaugh in his radio studio.

either. "That is a myth," he told his listeners. "That has been disproven at the World Health Organization and the report was suppressed. There is no fatality whatsoever. There's not even major sickness component associated with secondhand smoke." Limbaugh, a heavy smoker, died of lung cancer at age 70.

The first computers, developed during World War II, were huge, immovable cabinets that had

extraordinary data-crunching abilities for their time, though they were feeble by today's standards. They had the potential to solve an age-old problem. Denis Diderot, who in 1751 co-founded the first expansive encyclopedia, warned that more information appeared every year and eventually there would be too much to fit in an encyclopedia. But now, computers could store unlimited quantities of information, make it easily accessible, and even cross-reference it.

Even more was in store. Computers could become communication devices. In 1968 two psychologists who studied computers, Joseph Carl Robnett Licklider and Robert W. Taylor, wrote a paper titled "The Computer as a Communication Device." Like most early computer visionaries, they tended toward the extravagant and optimistic. "In a few years," they promised, "men will be able to communicate more effectively through a machine than face to face." Really? More rapidly, certainly, but why more effectively? What was meant by "effectively?"

The pioneers did not contemplate what a computer might do for a Father Coughlin, a Goebbels, a Rush Limbaugh, or a ruthless totalitarian regime such as China or Russia. The US military worried about the Russians and saw the development of the technology as a race against the Soviets, but they saw everything that way. Even they did not foresee the ways in which the Russians would attack the US with computer technology.

One year before a single computer communicated with a second one, Licklider and Taylor envisioned a vast network of computers all over the world in communication with each other. They wrote of what they called an "intergalactic computer network." They foresaw much of the modern world, including the use of graphics, digital libraries, e-commerce, online banking, and cloud computing.

On October 29, 1969, a computer at UCLA communicated with one at Stanford. The message traveling 350 miles was supposed to be LOGIN, but only LO came through. Improvements followed, and the network grew to 25 computers in the early 1970s.

Mark Zuckerberg, born prophetically in 1984, was one of a new generation for whom extensive computer networks were a part of life. Networks for online messaging were created. Social media began with Six Degrees in 1997, the name coming from the idea that any two people in the world have no more than six degrees of separation from one another. Lists of friends could be created for a personal bulletin board. Six Degrees grew to more than three million members. Online dating services became popular in the late 1990s and into the twenty-first century.

As a Harvard student, Zuckerberg created FaceMash, a rather insulting program rating people by their portraits.

This managed to offend most people, but then in 2004 he moved on to Facebook.

Tens of thousands of students in colleges around the country wanted to sign up. Three years later he was a billionaire. Today he is worth more than 100 billion dollars and Facebook has more than one billion users.

Wikipedia was launched in 2001 as an online encyclopedia. It had been Diderot's innovation to have each item written by different authorities, but in his conception, they were to be experts in their field. Anyone can contribute or edit a Wikipedia page, and there is no reliable way of evaluating the expertise of the contributors, who often use pseudonyms. Incorrect information is often posted, and once there it shows up in many other websites and posts. Wikipedia itself says that the threshold for including information is "verifiability, not truth"; a contribution does not meet the standard for inclusion unless it has been previously published in a "reliable source."

Errors in Wikipedia entries are **more often mistakes** than intentional lies, but they **soon become facts.** Wisely, numerous academic and journalistic **outlets do not accept Wikipedia as a source.** It does have one value, however. **An entry often** lists reputable sources, and you can go to these sources rather than trusting the Wikipedia entry itself.

IS WIKIPEDIA RELIABLE?

Life's Little Mysteries, a podcast series of LiveScience (like Wikipedia, a user-supported online project) asked Adam Riess, professor of astronomy and physics at Johns Hopkins University and one of the scientists credited with proposing the existence of dark energy, to rate Wikipedia's "dark energy" entry. "It's remarkably accurate," Riess said, "certainly better than 95 percent correct."

But when Life's Little Mysteries asked drummer Nate Donmoyer to look at the page about his indie pop band Passion Pit, he found ten factual errors ranging from subtle to significant. Some information even appeared to have been added to the page by companies or organizations in search of publicity. "It's kind of crazy," Donmoyer said. "I don't think I can trust Wikipedia again. The littlest white lies can throw its whole validity off."

I was once asked by a similar research project to assess the Wikipedia entry on Basques. I found it to be mostly but not entirely accurate. I have found this on most entries. The problem is that you don't know what to believe and what to discard.

There is a great deal of discussion on the internet and in academic and journalism circles about the accuracy of Wikipedia. Much of this discussion is on pages sponsored by Wikipedia, and Wikipedia entries get the most hits, but there have been several independent studies—easily located online, but most more than a decade old—comparing the accuracy of Wikipedia with encyclopedias created by credentialed contributors. The consensus seemed to be that Wikipedia was less accurate but not dramatically so.

I do not rely on information from Wikipedia because I've found important mistakes in its articles. You can do this too. Pick a subject you've been studying from primary sources and read the Wikipedia entry to see if it's right. Often I will find the same mistakes all over the internet, and I don't know if Wikipedia is creating or echoing those mistakes. I believe that Wikipedia is an honest effort, not a conspiracy to spread lies and disinformation. On the other hand, if lies and disinformation were on someone's agenda, it wouldn't be difficult to plant falsehoods on Wikipedia.

The courts, too, have questioned the accuracy of Wikipedia. In "State v. Flores," an unpublished decision by the Texas Court of Appeals for the 14th District dated October 23, 2008, the court refused the appellant's request to take judicial notice of a Wikipedia entry describing the "John Reid interrogation technique." The court reasoned in footnote 3 that Wikipedia entries are inherently unreliable because they can be written and edited anonymously by anyone.

Librarians and teachers advise students to use more than one source, try to ensure that the sources are reliable, look for tiebreakers in case of disagreement, and use the articles in encyclopedias in general and Wikipedia in particular as jumping-off points rather than final words. Seeking verification and considering the reliability of a source are the same tactics that can shield us from day-to-day lies.

Mobile phones, cell phones, developed slowly, starting in 1973. The early ones were large, clumsy, and expensive—certainly not something you could carry in your pocket. That changed in 2007 when Apple developed the iPhone, and social media took off.

The year before the iPhone's introduction, the Silicon Valley founders of Twitter chose their company name because its dictionary definition was "short bursts of inconsequential information" or "chirps of birds." The founders considered themselves great free-speech advocates.

With a smart phone you could chirp on the go. The problem with this and all social media is that it is ruled by friends, followers, and likes. The more of these you have, the more important you are. As Hitler pointed out, the bigger the lie, the more people it attracts. The wilder and more outrageous the statement, the more friends, followers, and likes it draws.

Facebook acknowledges this phenomenon but denies responsibility. Nick Clegg, a Facebook vice-president, said that "content that provokes strong emotions is invariably going to be shared," but he insisted that this was not in the nature of Facebook but was due to "human nature." People, not Facebook, caused the phenomenon, Facebook claimed.

A SOCIAL-MEDIA WHISTLEBLOWER

Social-media platforms were attacked in 2021 by one of their own, a 37-year-old former Facebook product manager. In interviews and congressional testimony, Frances Haugen claimed that Facebook put profits ahead of public safety. "The thing I saw at Facebook over and over again was that there were conflicts of interest between what was good for the public and what was good for Facebook, and Facebook over and over again chose to optimize for its own interests, like making more money," she said in a 2021 interview with the CBS news magazine show *60 Minutes*.

In a statement to a Senate subcommittee in October 2021, Haugen characterized Facebook as a "system that amplifies division, extremism, and polarization" around the world. "Facebook became a $1 trillion company by paying for its profits with our safety, including the safety of our children," she wrote. "And that is unacceptable."

Haugen accused Facebook of having research showing the harm that it does and concealing this from shareholders and the public. She told the US Senate, "I came forward because I recognized a frightening truth: Almost no one outside of Facebook knows what happens inside Facebook . . . . As long as Facebook is operating in the dark, it is accountable to no one. And it will continue to make choices that go against the common good."

The profit orientation of social media was demonstrated in the September 2021 Russian elections, when Google and Apple removed a smart voting app from their app stores. The app had provided a practical and safe way for Russians to vote against their ruling government. The Russian government led by Vladimir Putin argued that social media were interfering with Russian elections, and by aiding the opposition they were. But they folded not on a principle of noninterference but because the government threatened them with a loss of access to the profitable Russian market.

According to Haugen and other critics, social-media platforms frequently make such questionable decisions based on profit. But don't most corporations? Film companies reshape their content at the request of the Chinese government in order to have their films distributed in a huge and very profitable Asian market. US textbook publishers reshape content to gain approval by review boards in big states. Should social-media companies be held to a higher standard than other companies, or should all companies be held to a higher standard? Are the greedy misdeeds of social media more harmful than other corporate greed?

The Wall Street Journal examined the leaked Facebook documents and concluded, "Facebook Inc. knows, in acute detail, that its platforms are riddled with flaws that cause harm, often in ways only the company fully understands." According to the *Journal*, "Time and again, the documents show, Facebook's researchers have identified the platform's ill effects. Time and again, despite congressional hearings, its own pledges, and numerous media exposés, the company didn't fix them. The documents offer perhaps the clearest picture thus far of how broadly Facebook's problems are known inside the company, up to the chief executive himself."

According to Bloomberg, the leaked documents show Facebook staff who studied misinformation concluding that the social network's core products contribute to the spread of harmful material and that the company's efforts to eliminate misinformation are undermined by political considerations.

Haugen believes that social media's problems can be fixed. On her website she states, "We can have social media that brings out the best in humanity." There is a growing consensus that social media needs to be fixed. Exactly how to do that is a difficult and delicate question of managing the free flow of speech.

Twitter allowed people hungry for publicity, such as politicians and celebrities, to put out their messages without the fact-checking filter of journalism. Donald Trump was for years a kind of in-joke at *The New York Times* for his elaborate schemes to get coverage, sometimes with a pseudonym or an anonymous phone call. With Twitter he could just tweet.

Twitter founder Evan Williams was confident that "once everybody could speak freely and exchange information and ideas, the world was automatically going to be better." He later claimed to be disappointed, but he shouldn't have been surprised. If you open up a dialogue to everyone, the biggest liars and slickest hustlers will always move in.

Seventeenth-century French writer François de La Rochefoucauld, known for his maxims, wrote, "To succeed in the world we do everything we can to appear successful." This is where social media is a great gift. A barrage of false information and well-planted photographs can create a powerful illusion.

The power of illusion was a recognized tactic long before social media. It did not work for President George W. Bush when he declared victory in Iraq, but it worked for Lenin. The October 1917 uprising in Petrograd (now Saint Petersburg) that ushered in the Communist revolution was what some have called "the first lie of the Soviet Union." It wasn't the first, because Lenin and the Bolsheviks had told quite a few lies to get to that point, starting with the name Bolshevik, which means "the majority." Their

Russian actor Vasili Nikandrov as Vladimir Lenin in Sergei Eisenstein's *October*, a 1928 silent film that celebrated the 1917 October Revolution.

name gave them some standing—appearing successful leads to success—but they were not a majority. They were not even a majority of revolutionaries. The real revolution had been a spontaneous violent explosion in February in which Tsar Nicholas II was overthrown. The Bolsheviks had been unprepared at the time, few in number and out of money. Their leader, Vladimir Lenin, was not even in the country and played no part in the February uprising. He had to stage another revolution in which he appeared to be in charge, overthrowing the weak moderate leftist provisional government installed in the Winter Palace, the lavish historic residence of the tsars. But on that famous October day in 1917, the Red Guard, the troops he had organized for this coup, failed to rally. The Winter Palace remained in the hands of government. No one had been arrested. Restaurants and shops were open. Life seemed normal.

Then Lenin, from his headquarters across town, announced that a revolution had taken place and the Bolsheviks had established a worker state with worker-controlled production and the abolition of private property. His sleight of hand worked: Without any mass mobilization, with few street fights or barricades, and with few even participating, his desired outcome happened. Lenin appeared to be in charge—at least he said he was—and so, on the wings of a big lie, he was.

The visually rich 1928 film *October,* by Sergei Eisenstein, created an image of a huge, angry mob storming the Winter Palace. This never happened, but it became the lasting image of the October Russian Revolution.

Lenin's trick was astounding, so seemingly far-fetched

that even today most people believe the movie version **instead of the real event.** Today, with social media, pulling off success by the appearance **of success** is no great trick and is often accomplished.

And if you want it backed up by a film version, there is no need for the genius of an Eisenstein. Most anyone can post a staged video that will work.

When ISIS, the armed and violent group trying to establish an Islamic dictatorship—what they called a caliphate—first went on the attack in Northern Iraq, they made no effort to keep their movements secret, as military usually do. Instead they posted selfies on Instagram and videos and bold claims on Twitter and Facebook. Though outnumbered and outgunned, they seemed unstoppable on social media. This not only helped them recruit more volunteers from around the world, it enabled them to intimidate and defeat superior military forces. Then they used social media to publicize these unlikely wins. It couldn't last forever, but they had a streak of success. Hitler, back in the age of radio, said, "Artillery preparations before an attack as during the World War will be replaced in the future war by the psychological dislocation of the adversary through revolutionary propaganda." Social media is ideal for this, and warfare will probably never be the same.

The big difference between Orwell's nightmare and today's reality is that,

to date, government does not control the screens. In the novel, all screens were in the hands of Big Brother, the personification of the state. The world is moving ever closer to the Big Brother state, with thousands of cameras installed by police and governments to monitor public places. The Chinese state has come closest to this Orwellian world, though democracies are doing the same on a smaller scale.

By 2018 the Chinese government had installed 349 million surveillance cameras, five times the number in America, with more being added all the time.

In most of the world there is no Big Brother controlling the internet, but it is far from the free and open system it promised to be. Dictatorships routinely black out internet use. The Arab Spring, a series of uprisings in the Arab world starting in 2010, were greatly facilitated by the use of Facebook and Twitter. Some credited Facebook with the overthrow of the Egyptian government. But when the movement reached Syria, the dictatorship of Bashar al-Assad was able to shut down the internet on Fridays, the religious day in which the population went to mosques and organized protests.

A man carrying shopping bags blocks the path of Chinese tanks near Tiananmen Square, Beijing, on June 5, 1989. Students demanding freedoms of speech and press led demonstrations in the square between April 15 and early June that year. The suppression of the protests by the Chinese army killed hundreds or thousands of Chinese people and wounded thousands more. No discussion of the protests or massacre is permitted in China, in public or online. This anonymous man came to be known as "Tank Man." The photo was taken from the Beijing Hotel, about half a mile away, by AP photographer Jeff Widener.

When the internet emerged as a factor in Chinese life in the early 1990s, the Chinese Communist Party stepped in to control it. All internet connections had to run through state-run telecommunications companies. The ministry of public security started blocking information deemed inappropriate or subversive. International communication was severely restricted, and it remains so for China's 800 million internet users.

In 1998, China unleashed the Golden Shield project, a huge database containing personal information on more than a billion Chinese citizens. It monitors every electronically expressed thought in China. Censors and cyber police track every byte of information. Golden Shield also maintains a database of banned words such as the list of words that shuts down any discussion of Tiananmen Square. But the system does more than suppress what the government doesn't like. It has also been used to put out thousands of stories, lies that are the official versions of reality. Cell phone users are even forced to install an app for accessing and controlling their phones, and there are random checks to see if a phone still has the required app. The Chinese internet is a latter-day version of Nazi radios.

The standard Russian approach is different, aiming at "the annihilation of truth," as chess champion Kasparov put it. Russia has had pretty much the same secret police from tsarist times to Lenin's Cheka; then, in succession, the GPU, GPRU, and NKVD; then the KGB; and finally Vladimir Putin's FSB (Federal Security Service) today, which uses the same sword-and-shield emblem as the KGB of Communist times.

For all their changing initials, Russian secret police retain the same approaches and techniques and the same view of the power of lies. The more untruths the government can plant, the more confusion and chaos it can spread.

Russian Communists invented the word "disinformation," setting up a special agency for its spread in 1923. Stalin started using the word after World War II. During the Cold War, the KGB produced thousands of fake organizations and fake dissidents, false stories, and conspiracy theories to sow discord in the West. One of the most famous, thoroughly exposed and debunked but still alive in social media, is that the US military spread AIDS.

With its disinformation tradition, Russia was ready and eager to seize on the uses of social media. The FSB, set up after the 1991 collapse of the Soviet Union and strongly shaped by former KGB agent Putin, built a sprawling bureaucracy to spread disinformation on social media. An international broadcast radio network, RT, was established to spread disinformation via the airwaves around the world. Many American conspiracy theories have RT origins. The lie that Barack Obama was not born in the US was promoted by RT. The lie that Hillary Clinton was heading a child-molestation ring and the conspiracy theory that aircraft were secretly spreading poisons in their white condensation trails were promoted by the FSB.

Facebook acknowledged in 2017 that in the prior two years—

the election period— 126 million Americans, about three-quarters of

Facebook's American users, had been reading

Russian propaganda

on Facebook, in most cases

without realizing it.

The Russians argued both sides of race relations, gun control, abortion rights, and immigration. The goal was to make controversial issues more controversial.

In 2017 Angie Dixson appeared on Twitter as a ferocious defender of every lie told by Donald Trump and a fierce attacker of everyone who denounced his lies. It was a full-time job for Angie; whatever else she might do, she made time to tweet ninety times a day. Her name was curious, sounding vaguely like nearly forgotten 1960s movie and television star Angie Dickinson, but her Twitter profile picture was actually that of a model who was then dating actor Leonardo DiCaprio. Although ostensibly an American focusing on American issues, Angie periodically slipped into diatribes about Ukraine. Angie, who was really a Russian computer program, could not help herself. She did not exist; she was a "bot," short for robot. Once exposed, she vanished, but a new bot defending Angie and savaging the people who had exposed her appeared—another Russian bot.

A wholesome young American woman, Jenna Abrams reached online celebrity status with her commentaries on pop culture, mixed into which were right-wing lies such as a story about CNN offering pornography. *Variety* picked up that one. She was also quoted on various matters in *The New York Times* and *Washington Post*.

Anyone embarrassed by being duped by bots should take comfort in knowing that major media outlets fall for it too.

Jenna was a Russian bot. Some researchers, according to Carl T. Berg-strom and Jevin D. West, who studied this, estimate that half the traffic on the internet is generated by bots. It is not only governments with agendas, though much of it is. From Southeast Asia to the Balkans, poor kids are realizing substantial profits on what are called "click farms," pro-ducing huge quantities of bots that draw advertisers. They have found, as many have before them, that the more outrageous a lie, the more follow-ers it will attract. In 2018 alone, Facebook deleted almost three billion fake accounts, more than their total number of legitimate users.

Russian disinformation seeks opportunities to destabilize American life. In 2021, the State Department's Global Engagement Center, which monitors foreign disinformation, identified four publications that were secretly run by Russian intelligence and were questioning the reliability of Western Covid-19 vaccines. The publications said the vaccines had dangerous side effects and were carelessly rushed through the approval process. None of these accusations were true, and the four outlets had few readers, but building readership was not their goal. The plan is always to start quoting from these bogus studies on social media, and that, not the publications themselves, is what will spread the lies.

The 2016 US presidential election campaign unleashed an unprece-dented lying spree. Thousands of fake websites were suddenly born, each spinning lie after lie, and these lies then spread onto personal websites and networks.

Studies show that by autumn 2016, more fake stories than real ones were being shared on Facebook and Twitter. Social media became the principal source of lies. Lies are usually sexier than the truth, so traditional news outlets started to focus on the carnival. An estimated ten percent of news coverage examined policy positions of candidates.

P.W. Singer and Emerson T. Brooking, authors of *Like War: The Weaponization of Social Media* (2018) claimed that the networks—NBC, CBS, and ABC—spent a total of thirty-two minutes during the entire year discussing the positions of the candidates.

Researchers found 400,000 bots on Twitter in the 2016 election run-up, two-thirds of which were pro-Trump. Russian bots retweeted pro-Trump fake stories thousands of times. They also retweeted Trump tweets 469,537 times (that we know of).

It is unclear what effect this had on Trump winning the election. He lost the popular vote by 3 million votes and won the electoral college by gaining tiny margins in a few states.

A study by Nir Grinberg and other social scientists, published in *Science* magazine in 2019, claimed that only one percent of Twitter users—primarily conservative voters—were exposed to eighty percent of the fake news on Twitter.

In March 2021, US intelligence services released a declassified report on foreign interference in the 2020 election. The fifteen-page report contained no surprises. There was no attempt to interfere with the election process—to alter votes, voter registrations, or vote counts. However, the top echelons of the Russian government released stories of corruption by Joe Biden and tried to get news media to pick them up. This had worked against Hillary Clinton in 2016 but did not catch on in 2020. Donald Trump and his lawyer, Rudi Giuliani, echoed the Russian lies almost word for word. Meanwhile, Iran put out damaging material against Trump but could not bring themselves to boost the Biden campaign. Cuba, Venezuela, and the Lebanese-based militant Islamist group Hezbollah attempted to interfere on a small scale. Foreign interference in US elections is becoming a way of life.

It is also unclear how much of a role Russian bots had in Brexit—the 2016 vote on separating the United Kingdom from the European Union. There were bots on both sides, but the bots favoring an exit from the EU outnumbered the opposing bots by five to one. Only one percent of Twitter users were following this conversation, but the vote to exit only won by 52 to 48 percent.

Putin's faith in social-media disinformation seemed to fade in March 2022 as his invasion of Ukraine generated daily news coverage of the death and destruction he had unleashed. To keep the Russian people in the dark, he began to shut down social media platforms.

It would be a classic lie to claim that Russians are the fundamental **source of lies in the US. There is no shortage of** homegrown all-American liars.

QAnon is an example. Those deep in the right-wing conspiracy world believe Q is a person, someone in the government with top security clearance who knows what is really going on. He leaks classified information called "Q drops." Some think he is John F. Kennedy Jr., the son of the assassinated president. Never mind that John Jr. died in a plane crash in 1999. One website features a current picture of John Jr. looking like actor Pierce Brosnan with a gray beard and asserts that "the proof is overwhelming." It also shares the bad news that "he's the long forewarned–of anti–Christ figure."

Q takes risks. Being proved wrong is of no importance— at least it isn't boring, so it gets attention.

Q predicted that on October 17, 2020, John Jr. would show up in Dallas of all places (where his father was killed) and be announced as

Donald Trump's running mate, replacing Mike Pence, the classic "October surprise" to win the 2020 election. This was another lie without a future, like the weapons of mass destruction, but the fact that it never happened created no embarrassment. Whoever creates these Q drops must know that these things will be exposed and doesn't care.

QAnon promotes a lot of Jewish conspiracies. The 2018 Camp Fire in California, in which 85 people died, was not caused by Pacific Gas and Electric, as a real investigation concluded, but by the Jewish-controlled Rothschild Bank beaming solar energy from space. Accusing the Rothschilds of conspiring is a favorite antisemitic charge, in fact a bit old-fashioned, like much from QAnon.

Another QAnon theory holds that Jews are slipping people of color into white counties to unseat white majorities. Also, Jews were behind the 2018 shooting at Marjorie Stoneman Douglas High School in Florida that killed 17 and injured another 17. Such school shootings are frequently said to be hoaxes, because there is no other good answer to why this is not an argument for gun control.

More than two dozen congressional candidates in the 2020 election shared QAnon material or even appeared on QAnon shows. Most of them were not elected, but Marjorie Taylor Greene was elected to Congress from Georgia's solidly Republican fourteenth district after pushing QAnon theories, especially antisemitic ones. "There are too many coincidences to ignore," she said. She may or may not privately believe all this insanity. She got elected, so apparently it did not hurt her; perhaps in that district it helped her. Lying, even outrageously, does pay off sometimes. In Congress she was treated as a pariah and kept off committees. She began backing down and deleted statements from her website. Liars can be flexible. But she didn't back down much. In 2022 Twitter shut down her account because of the disinformation she was promoting, especially about the Covid pandemic.

Andrew Breitbart was a cofounder of *HuffPost* and the conservative *Drudge Report* website. In 2001 he became more conservative and got more attention with his extreme right-wing *Breitbart News*. In 2012, when he dropped dead from a heart attack at age 43, Steve Bannon, a former investment banker, took over the website and championed neo-Nazis and white supremacists.

Bannon became a top Trump advisor in 2016. Trump, by his own admission, doesn't read, but Bannon does. With Bannon as an advisor, Trump followed many of the standard protocols of dictators of the past, people Trump probably knew little about. "Make America Great Again" is a classic fascist statement. Hitler referred to Germany's mythic greatness, and Mussolini referred to the Romans. Creating confusion by flooding the airwaves with lies is a standard totalitarian approach, as is arguing both sides of something. Trump pursued the lie that Obama was not born in the US, then repudiated it, then backed it some more.

Calling the press "the enemy of the people" is another classic demagogue's tactic. The phrase itself was a standard line of Lenin.

Where was Trump getting all this from?

Creating distrust of the electoral system is yet another standard totalitarian tactic. Trump warned that the 2016 election would be fraudulent, and then, when he won, he still claimed he had been cheated out of winning the popular vote. He made the same warning in 2020, and after he lost, he claimed he had won "by a landslide" and the election had been stolen. After losing some sixty court cases—almost all of which were dismissed for a complete lack of evidence, even by the three Supreme Court judges he had nominated—his claim seemed a pointless exercise. Why would he pursue sixty cases with no evidence? As always, Trump was playing to his supporters, people well versed in conspiracy lies. He built a movement of people, including some elected Republicans, who would insist that elections could not be trusted. Always the huckster, he even raised millions of dollars from supporters for this cause. It all seemed worthwhile even without winning a single case.

Alex Jones is another prominent social media conspirator. Jones is the modern internet update on the traditional American con artist who used to go from town to town selling snake-oil cures that did nothing. Jones makes tens of millions of dollars selling his diet supplements and other phony products, such as a toothpaste that was supposed to prevent Covid-19. He sells much of this on Amazon, which makes millions of dollars for Amazon as well as himself. Jones makes clear that his money goes to his right-wing causes, which leads many to question why Amazon is in this business.

Jones, who became deeply involved in the sometimes-violent movement to overturn the 2020 election results, was sued by Connecticut parents for his claim that the 2012 killing of twenty first-graders and six school employees at a Sandy Hook elementary school was staged. He backed off and said that the mass shooting was real, but he also claimed that the lawyers suing him were engaged in child pornography. Keep creating chaos. In November 2021, the court found Jones and his Infowars website liable for defamation.

How did a respected intelligence officer, General Michael Flynn, degenerate into a crackpot liar? He was the first in US military intelligence to understand that the enemy was hiding in the open on social media, and he was hugely influential in changing the way intelligence operated. But he had a poor management style and was often resented; he was forced into retirement during Barack Obama's presidency, and he became an outspoken and bitter opponent of Obama. He also became entangled in dubious relations with the Turkish and Russian governments. In 2011 he started tweeting his ideas of foreign policy, which interested no one. Then his tweets started to change to hatred toward Muslims and Jews. He tweeted that Obama was a secret Muslim and Hillary Clinton was involved in sex crimes with children. If she was elected, she planned to outlaw Christianity. The more outrageous he became, the more Twitter fans he attracted. When he declared that the Washington elite regularly gathered to drink human blood and semen, he got 4,800 likes, one of his most successful tweets.

What is the nature of all these liars? Are they psychopaths who cannot help lying, or do they lie as a result of rational calculations? Often, if confronted, they will back off from their lies as Trump did about Obama's birthplace and Alex Jones did about Sandy Hook. How often do they believe the things they tweet or say? It is natural to think that they don't really believe Jews are sending rays from space or that John Kennedy Jr. is about to show up, but we don't really know.

After Nazi propaganda chief Goebbels **killed himself in 1945,** his diaries—which he had microfilmed before storing the originals in the Reich Chancellery—were found to be as full of lies **as his propaganda had been.** He lied to himself and to posterity as **well as his contemporaries.**

HOW A STABLE GENIUS LIED HIS WAY TO THE TOP

"Society is always prone to accept a person offhand for
what he pretends to be, so that a crackpot posing as a
genius always has a certain chance to be believed."
—Hannah Arendt

Donald Trump, while president, described himself as "so great looking and smart, a true stable genius." The adjective "stable" was added to counter the suggestion of anonymous staffers that Trump was mentally unstable, but genius is standard fare for aspiring dictators. After all, if lies are flying in every direction, who are you going to trust but the one genius in the room?

Hitler and Mussolini were also self-declared geniuses. North Korean leader Kim Jong-il claimed to be a genius, according to his own media, not only for his ability to build socialism but for his power to "stop the rain and make the sun come out."

But how did this particular genius, Donald Trump, come to power?

Trump, always rankled by the fact that he never won the popular vote, a fact he constantly lied about, went so far as to assert that his true mandate came from God. "Our rights are not given to us by men, our rights are given to us by our creator." His press secretary Sarah Sanders stated that God "wanted Donald Trump to be president and that's why he is here."

Trump had inherited a real estate fortune from his father and badly mismanaged it. By the age of 63 he had been through four bankruptcies, and the holding company for his hotels and casinos, drowning in $1.2 billion debt, banned him from their executive board. That was when he reinvented himself as a reality television star, and for a time that went well. But when his ratings slipped and he began to fade, he started using social media to promote his television appearances and his huckster products such as vitamins—another snake-oil con man like Alex Jones.

In 2011, though, his tweets started to change. Perhaps he was originally venting his frustrations when he started picking fights with people, calling them "losers" or "weak." "Sad" was another favorite tag. People who followed social media loved this new disagreeable persona. People of prominence just didn't talk like this. Grownups didn't talk like this. Trump quintupled his tweeting in 2011 and quintupled it again in 2012.

As his following grew, he became increasingly outrageous. He moved from attacking celebrities like comedian Rosie O'Donnell to more political targets such as China and Iran. And he started making disparaging remarks about people of color. He attracted the attention of white supremacists and what Steve Bannon called the "alt-right" (short for "alternative right," a term coined in 2008 by white supremacist Richard Bertrand Spencer). Although he had been a supporter of Barack Obama, he started to tear at him with the same viciousness once reserved for Rosie. He was becoming political, but he was carrying on in a way politicians never did. He found a following for this on social media. He created a website to suggest his candidacy for president. His outlandishness not only brought him internet followers but attention from news media, even if only to criticize him. A politician who talked like this was always good copy. Covering other politicians seemed boring by contrast. He had a far larger internet presence and far more coverage than any of his Republican opponents.

It became the model for his presidency as well. Impeached twice, losing the popular vote for reelection by a margin of seven million votes, and slinking off to Florida in disgrace, his presidency seemed no more successful than his real estate company or his television career. Was this a genius? You decide.

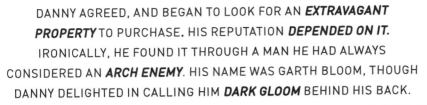

DANNY AGREED, AND BEGAN TO LOOK FOR AN **EXTRAVAGANT PROPERTY** TO PURCHASE. HIS REPUTATION **DEPENDED ON IT.** IRONICALLY, HE FOUND IT THROUGH A MAN HE HAD ALWAYS CONSIDERED AN **ARCH ENEMY**. HIS NAME WAS GARTH BLOOM, THOUGH DANNY DELIGHTED IN CALLING HIM **DARK GLOOM** BEHIND HIS BACK.

GARTH—WHO WAS CAMPAIGNING TO STOP CLIMATE CHANGE— SOMETIMES CALLED THE PRINCE OF REAL ESTATE "**DANNY THE DESTROYER**" BECAUSE OF DANNY'S **DELUXE, FUEL-HUNGRY AIRPLANES** AND HIS INVESTMENTS IN **COAL MINES AND OIL-FIRED ELECTRICITY.**

DANNY DIDN'T LIKE THIS NICKNAME AND WOULD OFTEN YELL . . .

GARTH IS THE **REAL DESTROYER**. HE'S OUT TO DESTROY ENERGY, REAL ESTATE, TRAVEL—**EVERYTHING WE LOVE!**

BUT IT WAS **THROUGH GARTH** THAT DANNY LEARNED OF A **LARGE MANSION** WITH THE WIDEST, **MOST PERFECT WHITE SAND BEACH** ON THE FLORIDA COAST.

THE LISTING PRICE WAS *INCREDIBLY LOW* BECAUSE *RISING SEA LEVELS AND STORMS* WERE PREDICTED TO INUNDATE AND DESTROY THE PROPERTY *IN A MATTER OF YEARS*. WHEN PROSPECTIVE BUYERS LEARNED ABOUT THIS, *THEY DISAPPEARED*.

BUT DANNY WAS MORE THAN HAPPY TO PURCHASE THE PROPERTY, BECAUSE HE THOUGHT *CLIMATE CHANGE* WAS A *HOAX*. TO HIM, THIS WAS A *GREAT OPPORTUNITY*, AND ANYONE WHO PASSED UP A DEAL LIKE THIS WAS A *FOOL*. DANNY ACQUIRED THE MANSION FOR A SONG, AND DIDN'T TELL ANYONE HOW *LITTLE HE PAID*. AFTER ALL, LOW-BUDGET DELUXE *WAS HIS SPECIALTY*.

TO BE CONTINUED . . .

CHAPTER NINE

PHOTOGRAPHIC LIES

Reality leaves a lot to the imagination.
—John Lennon

Who are you going to believe, me or your own eyes?
—Groucho Marx

The first chest, foot, or knee across the finish line might be difficult to determine in real time,

but a photo will reveal the winner without question. A camera set off by a tripwire or a more hi-tech approach, such as a movement sensor or photovoltaic cell, establishes irrefutable proof. "The photo never lies" is an old expression.

Courts of law, newspapers, and the public have accepted photographs as unshakable evidence of truth. But in truth, as long as there has been photography, some photographs have lied. It is far easier to make a photo lie today, with digital photography, than it was formerly with film. But it was always possible.

A photo in the Civil War placed Lincoln's head on a body that the photographer thought looked better. The Union and Confederate dead on Civil War battlefields, bloated and grotesque, were sometimes made to look more acceptable.

Robert Capa, one of the most celebrated photojournalists but also a mysterious figure whose real name wasn't Robert Capa, was accused of staging a famous 1936 photo of a soldier being shot in the Spanish Civil War. Modern examination shows the photo to have been taken some miles from where it was supposed to be; it is not certain that there was even any fighting at the true photo site. Joe Rosenthal of the Associated Press was accused of staging his famous photo of the American flag being raised on Mount Suribachi by US Marines during the 1945 battle

Robert Capa's photo of the death of a Republican militiaman in early September 1936.

with the Japanese for the island of Iwo Jima. This turned out to be a misunderstanding, although it is true that the flag he photographed was the second one raised on the spot, replacing a smaller one that did not show well in photographs.

In 1920 Sir Arthur Conan Doyle, creator of the brilliant fictional detective Sherlock Holmes,

was fooled by faked photographs of fairies, extraordinary in itself because you would have to believe that fairies existed to trust these photographs.

In 1917 ten-year-old Frances Griffiths, living in rural England, liked to walk into streams and come home soaking wet. When asked what she was doing, she explained that she was playing with fairies. Her

16-year-old cousin Elsie Wright, defending her from angry adults, made two photos of Frances—one with tiny winged women in loose gowns dancing around her shoulders, and the other with a gnome.

These pictures became part of family lore, and two years later Elsie's mother showed them at a meeting of the Theosophical Society, a popular English club of the time that investigated the paranormal. The society was intrigued and passed the photos to their group and talked about them, which is how they came to the attention of Arthur Conan Doyle in 1920. He approached the photos with the open-mindedness and cynicism one would expect

Elsie Wright's first photo of Frances Griffiths playing with fairies.

from the creator of Sherlock Holmes. He said that the photos might be "the most elaborate and ingenious hoax ever played upon the public," but he also conceded that they might be "epoch-making."

Doyle partnered with Edward Gardner of the Theosophical Society to investigate. Gardner was a prominent figure, known for lectures and writing on paranormal. It is not clear where he gained his expertise, but he warned Doyle that they had to move quickly because only young, innocent girls could see fairies, and once they were no longer teenagers—once Elsie, who was by then 19, fell in love—their fairy-viewing powers would be gone.

The photos were submitted to two photographers. One said **they were faked,** so Doyle and Gardner went with the second one, who said they **were authentic.**

But the girls did seem to be losing their powers. In 1920 they were only able to capture fairies in three photos, and in 1921 they were unable to produce any at all, although a psychic who followed them reported seeing several—a few, not a lot. Elsie complained that as she got older, fairies looked increasingly transparent and hard to see.

Doyle considered himself a man of science, but he was also engaged by the spiritualism that was fashionable at the time. He believed that there were fairies and that they vibrated too quickly for most of us to be able to see them. He also believed that young girls had special powers that faded with age.

The general public, even Elsie's father, were appalled that Doyle, a supposedly brilliant man, would be taken in by these girls and their silly hoax. But he had the photos, and they confirmed what he wanted to believe. Many agreed with Doyle, and even today some believe the photos are real. In 1982 Elsie described how she had cut the fairies from cardboard with her aunt's sewing shears and stuck them together with hat pins. It was supposed to be a hoax played on her parents, but strangers asked her about the fairy photos for the rest of her life.

Doyle had believed what he wanted to be true.

Faith in photographs as a source of truth grew during much of the twentieth century,

only to be destroyed by the end of the century. A growing belief in the importance of photographs was dramatized in the 1948 Twentieth Century Fox film *Call Northside 777*, which was based on a 1932 murder conviction in Chicago that was overturned eleven years later. James Stewart played a reporter trying to overturn the murder conviction. His key evidence was a photograph that showed a newspaper with the date on it, proving that a key witness had lied. Adding to the drama, the photo was in a different city, but he was able to get it to Chicago on time by means of a new technology that transmitted photographs electronically.

In the key scene, the photo image gradually appears on photosensitive blank paper spinning on a drum in Chicago. The case is proven and the falsely convicted prisoner is released.

This dramatization was a Hollywood expression of the near-universal enthusiasm for photographic techniques at the time. In the real-life story on which the movie was based, the eleven-year-old sentence was overturned without photography playing a role.

But there was also a growing cynicism about photography. Once Stalin saw the usefulness of an airbrush, a hand-held tool that sprays paint with compressed air, he regularly directed adjustments to be made to photographs. A photo of a demonstration during the 1917 revolution showed a shop sign in the background advertising gold and silver clocks. But in a retouched archival photograph the sign said, "You'll take what's yours through struggle," and an unreadable sign now clearly read, "Down with the monarchy."

Stalin not only made millions of people disappear from real life, he made people disappear from photos too.

Leon Trotsky, one of the key Russian Communist leaders, fell from grace in the 1920s and was forced into exile. His face disappeared from photographs of the revolution in which he had played a prominent role. An 1897 photograph of six men in a meeting with Lenin became five men meeting with Lenin once Alexander Malchenko was eliminated. In 1930 Malchenko was accused of being a spy and was executed, and after that he was no longer in the photo. Two others who had sided with Trotsky, Alexei Rykov and Lev Kamenev, were tried for treason in Stalin's Great Purge of 1936 and were executed. Both men had been Lenin deputies and acting Soviet Union premiers in the 1920s, but both disappeared from a 1922 photo with Lenin and other leaders. Rykov's portrait had even appeared on a 1924 *Time* magazine cover, but he was no longer seen in Russian photos.

Other dictators including Mao Zedong, Adolf Hitler, and Benito Mussolini also manipulated photographs. But it was a slow, painstaking process carried out in secret darkrooms. Today it is fast and easy, especially with digital images. Dating sites, social media, online auctions, fashion magazines, political campaigns, news tabloids, and even scientific journals feature manipulated photographs fairly often. The notion that you can take a photograph at face value seems quaint and out of date.

Manipulating digital photographs on social media has become so easy that it has degenerated to silliness or just to have fun. There are apps that allow you to do strange things to faces. In 2021, when a huge

Vladimir Lenin (seated at center) with fellow members of the League of Struggle for the Emancipation of the Working Class in 1897. Alexander Malchenko (standing at left, behind Lenin's right shoulder) was airbrushed out of this photo by Stalin years later.

container ship got stuck and blocked the Suez Canal, an app was created with an aerial photo of the ship blocking the canal. You could make the ship larger or smaller and move it to another photo to block something else. "Get it stuck in a swimming pool or across the entire Atlantic Ocean," the app suggested.

Manipulating photos
has become commonplace, a technology
available to anyone.

In 2021, students at Bartram Trail High School in St. Johns, Florida, were outraged to discover that the graduation photos of 80 girls had been altered without their knowledge in the school yearbook to cover up or reduce cleavage.

Faked photos have become common for all types of false claims. Dinesh and Tarakeshwari Rathod, two 30-years-olds, a married couple who were constables in the Maharashtra, India, police force, claimed to have summitted Mount Everest, and they had photos to prove it. The accomplishment got attention because they were the first Indian couple to have reached the summit. But then it was noticed that in the photos taken while they were climbing, they were wearing different gear than in the summit photos. Costume changes are not possible on sub-freezing Everest. On closer inspection, other odd crops and insertions were noticed. Nepalese experts ruled the photo a fake, and the couple was banned from climbing in Nepal for ten years.

Sometimes faked photos are simply silly. The family of Senator Mitt Romney dressed in shirts with a letter on each so that they could stand in a line and spell "R–O–M–N–E–Y," but someone using Photoshop rearranged them to spell "M–O–N–E–Y."

Manipulating photos to humiliate President Donald Trump was a favorite pastime. A photo was altered to make his pot belly even bigger, another to make it look like he had wet his pants. Some are more malevolent but speak to underlying truths—Trump with the KKK at a cross burning or with his arm around sex offender Jeffrey Epstein, kissing him. The latter example is a particularly bad Photoshop job. The Epstein shot was taken from a photo of Trump holding and kissing his daughter when she was 13, but Epstein's image was too big. It was shrunk, but then his body became too small for his head, and a shock of the girl's hair was inadvertently left in next to Epstein's head. But like so much on social media, there is little concern for whether you believe it or not. Trump did know Epstein and spoke supportively of white supremacists, so these were faked photos in service to true points. Is lying to assert the truth ever a worthwhile practice?

In 2017, when San Francisco quarterback Colin Kaepernick led a movement of NFL players to drop to a knee during the national anthem to protest police brutality, there was an effort to say that these football players were unpatriotic and were insulting the United States. A photograph was posted on Facebook, and then on Twitter, by a largely unknown group called "Vets for Trump." The photo showed the Seattle Seahawks in their locker room. Defensive lineman Michael Bennet, an outspoken advocate of the take-a-knee movement, was shown waving a burning American flag while teammates and the coaching staff cheered him on.

The photo was widely shared. This, it was implied, was the kind of thing that went on in the NFL behind closed doors. Except that no such flag burning ever happened. The real photo, taken two years earlier, showed the team doing their traditional victory dance celebrating an important win. It had been tweeted in 2016. The burning flag was added later. If you look carefully, the fraud can be seen. Something is off about the way Bennet is holding the flag. And that room has a sprinkler system that would have been set off by flames. The evidence is there, if you think about it, like the change of clothes on Mount Everest. But who looks that carefully at a photograph? It seems that we need to start doing exactly that.

In the 2016 election, expecting to lose or possibly wanting to cause distrust of elections regardless of the outcome, Trump started talking about election fraud. "I'm afraid the election is going to be rigged," he said. He presented no evidence, though he said he was hearing more and more about it. He didn't say who he was hearing this from.

Then Cameron Harris, a 23-year-old Maryland Republican, discovered—actually invented—something shocking. He said tens of thousands of fraudulent votes for Hillary Clinton were found in an Ohio ware-house. He later said that he had chosen Ohio because Trump had spoken about election fraud while in Ohio. Still, it was an odd choice, because even the Clinton camp knew that Trump would easily win Ohio.

Harris invented a story about a make-believe electrical worker's chance discovery of boxes of ballots pre-marked for Clinton. He knew his scam would be popular because it coincided with what Trump was saying, so Trump supporters would like it. He calculated correctly. He said the scam netted him about $100,000 in advertising revenue.

When journalists discovered his ruse, Harris was at first hesitant to talk about it because he was trying to build a political consulting business and was not sure creating fake news would be good for his business.

He created Randall Prince of Columbus, Ohio, an electrical worker who supposedly wandered into what he said was a little-used building and found the boxes. Harris said it was "a massive operation designed to deliver Clinton the crucial Swing State"—except that Ohio was not a swing state, it was a solid Republican state.

Google-searching for a photograph to use, he found one from the *Birmingham Mail* in England that showed a man standing behind black plastic boxes during a British election count. They might have been any boxes, but they were clearly labeled "Ballot Box." Harris simply wrote a new caption, "Mr. Prince shown here, poses with his find, as election officials investigate." He posted this on his fictitious news site, *Christian News, CTN.*

The first clue of fake news is a lack of specifics. Who was investigating, and in what way? "The story is still developing, and CTN will bring you more when we have it," he reported. It was an echo of Trump saying that he was hearing of voter fraud but not saying where. Lack of verifiable details should set off warning lights unless, like Sir Arthur Conan Doyle with the fairies, it is what you want to hear. Harris created six additional Facebook pages to help push things along. According to CrowdTangle, which tries to track audiences, six million people shared this revelation. How many millions were convinced they had seen absolute photo proof that Clinton rigged the election—never mind the fact that Trump comfortably won the state?

Harris told *The New York Times*, "At first it kind of shocked me… how easily people would believe it." An investigation found the story to be a fraud, and it was refuted by the Ohio Secretary of State.

Money was the motive.
Harris and other news fakers said they would have
been happy to promote Clinton and
attack Trump, but that was
not as profitable.

Trump supporters were a better market, much more willing to get behind fake news stories. But the fake news market may be shrinking, because Google is trying to keep ads off sites that are clearly fake news.

Voter fraud continued in 2020. A video was widely seen showing someone burning Trump ballots. The "ballots" can be seen to be from Virginia Beach, Virginia, but election officials there said these were samples and not real ballots. No one ever found out who was burning the fakes.

After the 2020 election, CNN—much disliked by Trump—was featured in a viral video in which host John King reported election results (which showed Trump losing) while trying to cover up with his hand an ad that showed the sponsorship of Pornhub, a popular distributor of pornographic videos. The video was a digitally engineered fake. Pornhub is not a CNN sponsor and their logo never appeared on the CNN screen, but 6.5 million viewers saw it there anyway.

On July 17, 2014, Malaysia Airlines flight MH17 from Amsterdam en route to Kuala Lumpur disappeared with 238 passengers, including 80 children and 15 crewmembers, over a section of Ukraine controlled by heavily armed Russian-backed separatists. A Dutch-led investigation determined that the plane had been shot down by a Russian missile that was traced to Russian operatives connected to Russian intelligence. The Russians denied everything and tried to manipulate Wikipedia's MH17 page to eliminate any mention of Russia. Various postings claim the Malaysian airline was at fault or that it was shot down by Ukrainians and innocent Russians were being victimized by a smear campaign. Then the Russians came up with a photo clearly showing that the Malaysian flight was fired on by a Ukrainian fighter jet.

This image aired on Russian state television appears to be a satellite photo of a Ukrainian jet (shown in the enlarged inset at right) shooting down the flight MH17 passenger plane, but the photo was quickly exposed as a fake, stitched together from a number of online images.

This photo was not one of Russia's finest works, but in truth, despite digital technology, most faked photos have clear giveaways. This one was supposed to be a satellite image, but the background showed it to be a composite of several satellite images. The attack plane was not the type they were claiming, and the MH17 image was a clumsy Photoshop product. When it turned out that the Russian engineer who had validated the photo did not even have an engineering degree, the Russian

Union of Engineers explained that they had gotten the photo "from the internet." The Russian internet offered several other explanations, often contradicting each other. Forget the Ukrainian fighter, according to one explanation, it was a Ukrainian surface-to-air missile. How could Russian intelligence be so clumsy? Because their goal was not so much to offer a plausible explanation but to spread confusion.

In 2008 the Iranian government released to the world a photo of four test missiles

being fired successfully. One of the four had actually failed, but it was replaced in the photo by a cloned photo of a successfully launched missile. This particularly clumsy clone was quickly detected, but cloning techniques are getting better.

After the 2020 assassination by drone of a leading Iranian figure, Qassem Soleimani, Fox News producer Yonat Frilling posted to Twitter a photo of graffiti on a wall in Iran that said in Farsi, "Thank you Trump." Frilling said this was from a protected source. Anyone who knew Iran found it odd that the Iranian people would cheer the murder of a figure as popular as Soleimani; even Iranians who are not government supporters don't like the idea of America bombing or assassinating their leaders. The photo, if real, would have been a considerable triumph for Donald Trump. It initially went viral in right-wing circles, but problems were revealed under closer scrutiny, and Frilling deleted the tweet.

The photo had originally been posted long before the drone attack. The earliest known posting was in 2018 to the Twitter account of Heshmat Alavi, though there may be earlier postings. Alavi claims to be an activist opposed to the Iranian government, and he has supposedly written articles for extreme-right websites and also for *Forbes*. No one seems able to find him, however, and *The Intercept*, an online magazine, ran an article with two sources claiming that Alavi is not a real person but a bot run by an Iranian opposition group, Mojahedin-e-Khalq (MEK), out of Albania. Hassan Heyrani, who claims to be a high-ranking operative for MEK, said, "They write whatever they are directed by their commanders and use this name to place articles in the press. This is not and has never been a real person." It is not clear who stole the graffiti photograph and posted it in connection with the 2020 assassination.

In 2020 Trump's operatives mounted a Facebook ad campaign in which his claim to represent "public safety vs. Chaos and Violence" was repeated in conjunction with a photo of a violent protest. But the photo of protestors clashing with police was actually a 2014 shot from Ukraine.

Techniques for manipulating photos are rapidly improving, but techniques for detecting photo fraud, the field of photo forensics, are improving too.

Most disinformation, conspiracies, and fake news do not bother being highly sophisticated about faking photographs. Often they are patched together from several posted images; by Googling the subjects, the components of a composite photo can be found. Is everything in the picture lit the same way and from the same light source? Do all the shadows line up consistently? It would be extremely rare for any two photos to have the exact same lighting. Do the depth of field and clarity of background match for the entire photo? Parallel lines, for example the two sides of a street, should merge in the distance at what is called the vanishing point, a dot that may or may not be in the picture frame. But whether in the frame or not, if two lines that appear to be parallel never meet, they are not from the same photo.

When an artist draws the sun, it is often depicted as a circle with lines or rays sticking out all around it. This is an artist's rendering of what really happens when a camera is pointed into a very strong light like the sun. It is called a lens flare. But all these rays must come from the same light in the same way or there has been some tampering. A false flare is easy to detect.

The pixels, the components of a digital photo, can be examined to see if some parts of the picture have been shrunk or enlarged to fit. For more sophisticated investigators, there is metadata, hidden information about the photo. Sometimes it is possible to identify the type of camera, even the owner, and the settings at which it was shot. Is everything in the photo shot with the same camera at the same settings? Techniques for exposing faked photos are growing increasingly sophisticated, but much of that skill is unnecessary because often the fakers are not trying that hard.

Another advantage of this technology is that it can verify real photos that come under attack. A great many conspiracy claims are based on the accusation that a photo has been faked. The famous moon-landing photo can be shown to be real. A favorite conspiracy theory about the assassination of President John Kennedy also focused on an alleged photo manipulation. The Kennedy assassination challenged investigators in numerous ways. The alleged killer, Lee Harvey Oswald, did not get to speak other than shouting a denial to the press as he was arrested. Jack Ruby, a terminally ill man with underworld connections, shot and killed Oswald. A government commission left issues unresolved. There is a photo of Oswald in his backyard with a holstered sidearm, holding the rifle with which he allegedly shot Kennedy. It has been claimed that since the shadow cast by his nose

This person is someone you might like to know, but she is not real. Her face was created by artificial intelligence using an algorithm that samples and recombines a huge database of real images. The image comes from ThisPersonDoesNotExist.com, which generates a new face from scratch each time you refresh the site.

points in a different direction than the shadow cast by his body, and an outdoor photograph cannot have two light sources, Oswald's head must have been placed on someone else's gun-toting body.

Fifty years after the assassination, forensic experts were able to construct a three-dimensional model showing that there were no inconsistencies in the lighting. There is no evidence of Photoshopping. This does not finally resolve the question of who killed JFK, but it does debunk one piece of evidence from conspiracy theorists.

The bad news for people who'd like to trust photographs is a new algorithm called "adversarial machine learning."

The problem with bots used to be that a photograph of the user was expected, and there were no photographs of nonexistent people. That was why Jenna Abrams had to borrow the face of Leonardo DiCaprio's girlfriend. But someone might recognize such a photo—someone like the real person, for example. The new algorithm, however, can invent very lifelike faces, so it is no longer necessary for a scammer to borrow a real facial photo.

THE PRINCE OF REAL ESTATE – PART 2: A GREAT DEAL OF **FREE PUBLICITY** AND ATTENTION WAS GIVEN TO THE **NEW LUXURY RESORT** OPENED BY THE FAMOUS DANNY DELUX. AS HE HAD HOPED, PEOPLE NOW BELIEVED THAT RUMORS OF HIS FINANCIAL COLLAPSE WERE **OBVIOUSLY FALSE**. WEALTHY PEOPLE WANTED TO BE **AMONG THE FIRST** TO VACATION AT DANNY'S MANSION, WHICH HE CALLED **THE CASTILLO**—THE CASTLE.

THE CASTILLO WAS **COMPLETELY BOOKED** UNTIL IT WAS **HIT BY A SEVERE HURRICANE** TOWARD THE END OF ITS FIRST SEASON. AFTERWARD THE BEACH **SEEMED SMALLER**.

GARTH SAID THE BEACH WAS BEING DROWNED BY RISING SEA LEVELS **CAUSED BY CLIMATE CHANGE** AND DANNY WOULD SOON BE **DANNY DRIFTWOOD**.

DANNY SAID THAT HURRICANES **SOMETIMES REMOVE SAND FROM BEACHES** AND THAT'S **ALL IT WAS**; CLIMATE CHANGE HAD NOTHING TO DO WITH IT. BUT GARTH POINTED OUT THAT THE HURRICANE HAD BEEN **INTENSIFIED** BY CLIMATE CHANGE.

HA! JUST A FEW DAYS AGO, THE NORTHEAST WAS **FREEZING COLD**.

THAT PROVES THE **CLIMATE ISN'T WARMING**. I'M RAISING MY RATES!

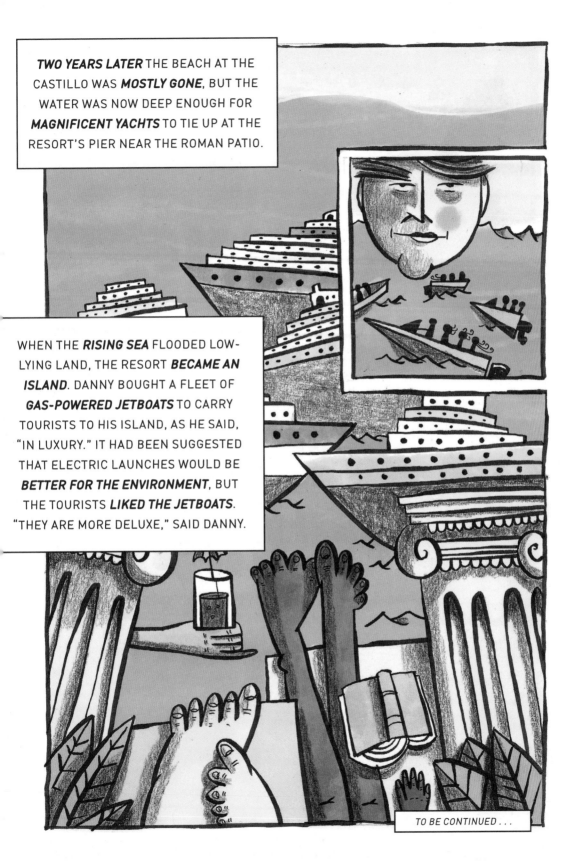

TWO YEARS LATER THE BEACH AT THE CASTILLO WAS *MOSTLY GONE*, BUT THE WATER WAS NOW DEEP ENOUGH FOR *MAGNIFICENT YACHTS* TO TIE UP AT THE RESORT'S PIER NEAR THE ROMAN PATIO.

WHEN THE *RISING SEA* FLOODED LOW-LYING LAND, THE RESORT *BECAME AN ISLAND*. DANNY BOUGHT A FLEET OF *GAS-POWERED JETBOATS* TO CARRY TOURISTS TO HIS ISLAND, AS HE SAID, "IN LUXURY." IT HAD BEEN SUGGESTED THAT ELECTRIC LAUNCHES WOULD BE *BETTER FOR THE ENVIRONMENT*, BUT THE TOURISTS *LIKED THE JETBOATS*. "THEY ARE MORE DELUXE," SAID DANNY.

TO BE CONTINUED . . .

CHAPTER TEN

SAVING CHILDREN: A BEST-LOVED LIE

An unexciting truth may be eclipsed by a thrilling falsehood.
—Aldous Huxley, *Brave New World Revisited*

Pedophilia, the sexual abuse of children, was a favorite false accusation long before the internet age, because no one is more feared and hated than someone who abuses children. Unsurprisingly, pedophilia has become a persistent theme in social media, a popular if not very original conspiracy theory.

Science in the hands of people who care little for facts can be a dangerous lie. A QAnon-promoted story spread across social media in 2020—on TikTok, YouTube, Instagram, and other platforms—about "global elites" kidnapping children and draining their blood to harvest the chemical adrenochrome for psychedelic experiences and to keep themselves young and strong. Not only was the lie spread on social media, but Philip McGraw, who holds a PhD in clinical psychology and hosted *Dr. Phil,* a television show claiming to be a forum for mental health issues, had a guest on his show in 2020 who alleged that her daughter had been kidnapped and tortured for adrenochrome.

Who were these "global elite?" This is a catch phrase for people who are educated and well-informed, the enemy of the conspirators—the kind of people who might call a lie a lie. Anyone who seems successful is in the elite. If you are reading this book you are probably elite, since the elite read books. This is why demagogues often brag about not reading books. There is particular venom for celebrities, for whom the adjective "Hollyweird" often turns up in social media. Some posts list celebrities with the words "arrested & under house arrest" next to the names. Some say "arrested & executed." It seems to be of no importance that such lies are easily proven false.

It was Q's contention that the only way you can achieve the fame that top celebrities enjoy is by doing something depraved. If you are rich and famous, surely you have been abusing children. The rich and famous are exactly the kind of people who kill children and harvest their adrenochrome.

Millions saw these posts, though they were based on absolutely nothing. The principal source was QAnon. Those putting out the child-abuse rumors formed a "Child Lives Matter" group pretending to defend these nonexistent child victims.

Adrenochrome really is a chemical found in the human body. There were studies in the 1950s about the possible role of the chemical in schizophrenia, and some writers in the mid-twentieth century, especially Aldous Huxley, became fixated on the idea that adrenochrome might be a new psychotropic drug. Psychotropic drugs are mood-altering, and many are available to treat depression, schizophrenia, bipolarity, anxiety, and other disorders. Such drugs are sometimes abused for recreational purposes.

But scientists who studied adrenochrome found very little of interest. It is a byproduct of adrenaline and can be purchased, so it is not necessary to kidnap children to get it. In Hunter S. Thompson's most famous book, *Fear and Loathing in Las Vegas* (1971), and in the 1998 movie adaptation, a writer and his attorney in Las Vegas experiment with various drugs including adrenochrome, and from this fiction comes the myth that adrenochrome "makes pure mescaline seem like ginger beer," as well as the lie that the only way to obtain it is from the adrenal gland of a living human.

Adrenal gland? Blood? The story keeps changing. One conspiracy theorist, Liz Crokin, said, "Adrenochrome is a drug that the elites love. It comes from children. The drug is extracted from the pituitary gland of tortured children. It's sold on the black market. It's the drug of the elites. It is their favorite drug."

One theorist went so far as to claim that Hillary Clinton and her aide Huma Abedin were caught on tape tearing off a child's face, wearing it as a mask, and drinking the child's blood to obtain adrenochrome. But no one can find such a tape.

Around 2014, with the help of QAnon, myths about the chemical were tied to old claims that Jews harvested children's blood. By 2017 it was being said that the Pixar film *Monsters, Inc.* was secretly about adrenochrome harvesting. A video circulated online with the title "Adrenochrome: The Elite Secret Superdrug." Though some platforms took this down, it reappeared in other places.

During the Covid-19 lockdown, celebrities were said to be going through adrenochrome withdrawal because the pandemic was making the necessary child trafficking more difficult, reducing the supply. The singer Lady Gaga was said to be engaged in child blood rituals to get the chemicals.

Placing false claims on celebrity pages made them more visible and helped to spread the lies. There is no evidence of any use for adrenochrome nor of anyone harvesting the chemical in any way, but that does not stop the story from spreading.

JEWISH BLOOD LIBEL

Rumors that Jews ritually murder children, often to obtain blood for Passover, a holiday that in reality involves no blood, first circulated in Europe in the twelfth century. Like many successful lies, this one kept fading out and resurfacing. It is back on the internet today.

In the late nineteenth century, for unclear reasons, this absurd medieval lie reappeared in Central Europe. There were some hundred cases of Jews being accused of murdering children for their blood, about a half-dozen of which went to trial. The courts rejected all the claims, but the idea spread, much as Donald Trump's election lie kept spreading despite its repeated refutations in court.

The most famous trial was in 1913 in the Ukrainian city of Kyiv, which, at the time, was part of the Russian tsarist empire. In 1911, 13-year-old Andrei Yushchinsky was found dead in a cave on the edge of the city, the victim of more than forty stab wounds. A right-wing Russian group, The Black Hundred—promoters of *The Protocols of the Elders of Zion* and many other antisemitic lies and organizers of the massacres of thousands of Jews, the so-called pogroms—announced that the boy had been ritually murdered by Jews.

Mendel Beilis, a 37-year-old father of five, was accused of the crime because he was Jewish and worked in a nearby brick factory. There was no evidence against him, but he spent two years in prison awaiting trial. The prosecution presented a bizarre array of witnesses—a pathologist bribed by the tsar, a drunken couple who gave conflicting accounts and then recanted everything when sober, a drunk who denied knowing anything, and the leader of a crime organization, Vera Cheberyak, who had blinded her lover for betraying her to the police. She was also suspected of killing her own son to keep him from talking.

The trial was protested around the world. In the US, the cause was taken up by leading social reformers including Jane Addams, the feminist and peace activist, and Booker T. Washington, the slave-born leader of the African American community.

Surprisingly, a jury of Ukrainian peasants, selected to assure conviction, found Beilis not guilty. But the Beilis myth lived on and was strongly featured in Nazi propaganda decades later. After World War II, 42 Jews, mostly concentration camp survivors, were killed in the Polish town of Kielce by a mob accusing them of killing children for blood. The Bishop of Lublin, Stefan Wyszynski, who was later named cardinal primate of Poland, declined to condemn the attack as antisemitic, saying that "during the Beilis trial the matter . . . was not definitively settled."

◇◇◇

Internet conspiracy theorists have targeted talk show host Ellen DeGeneres as well. Eric Trump, Donald Trump's son, stated on social media that DeGeneres, Barack Obama, and Hillary Clinton were all part of the "deep state," a conspiracy fantasy that was much loved by Trump, his supporters, and QAnon. The deep state, they told us, is a secret group of insiders plotting against us—we, the people. DeGeneres was an odd target because, aside from advocating for gay rights, she is not politically active. She is an outspoken lesbian activist for LGBTQ rights and in 2015 launched a line of home furnishings on Wayfair, an on-line furniture company that promotes equality and rights.

Conspiracy-promoters announced on Twitter that DeGeneres was involved in trafficking children and that her furniture sales were a coded coverup for this activity. They suggested on Reddit that the names of her items were actually names of missing children. One post said, "@ TheEllenShow please explain why you're selling pillows on Wayfair for over 10k with missing children's names on them? Are you a part of #wayfairtrafficking???" More and more accusations were posted, some accusing her of involvement with harvesting adrenochrome.

At the beginning of 2020, on Twitter and other social media, DeGeneres was said to be under house arrest for sex trafficking. The same posts claimed that Oprah Winfrey, the billionaires Bill and Melinda Gates, and Bill and Hillary Clinton were also under house arrest for the same crime. Thousands of people shared these posts. One tweet showed a photo of DeGeneres and asserted that the man standing behind her was a police officer in charge of her arrest. Actually, it was her producer, Andy Lassner.

Being exposed by facts is not a problem on social media. People saw it, and some believed.

Trump supporters spread increasingly absurd lies during the 2016 election campaign about Donald Trump's opponent, Hillary Clinton. It was Trump's idea of a political campaign. Nothing was too outrageous or too far-fetched. The more absurd the lie, the faster it spreads, and you never know who might believe it.

In this context, perhaps it was inevitable that the old medieval blood libel lies, that children were being murdered, would resurface. With only a few weeks remaining in the campaign, it became well-known, if not necessarily believed, that Hillary Clinton operated a child-trafficking ring out of a popular pizza parlor in Washington, DC. The story began when WikiLeaks released hacked emails of John Podesta, Clinton's campaign chairman. Right-wing social media, including a Reddit forum and an extremist 4chan message board, began scouring the released emails for clues to wrongdoing. Surely the emails contained something incriminating; otherwise, why were they stolen?

Podesta liked to cook and often talked about Italian food. That seemed suspicious. The right-wingers found communications with James Alefantis, who not only owned a popular DC pizzeria, Comet Ping Pong, but supported Democrats. Podesta mentioned "cheese pizza."

Aha! Why would Podesta be talking to a pizzeria about cheese pizza? 4chan proclaimed that cheese pizza was a code for "c.p.," used by pedophiles to mean child pornography.

The scene of the alleged crime, Comet Ping Pong, offered ping pong tables and long tables for eating pizza family-style. Anyone could go to this warm and crowded family restaurant and see that there was nothing nefarious taking place.

> # But there is no defense against an accusation this irrational, because denying it makes you look silly. To deny it you have to acknowledge it, and that gives it a perverse sort of credibility.

The story was soon labeled Pizzagate (as in, a Watergate-type scandal with pizza, the scandal that would take down Hillary).

Because anyone without the slightest knowledge on the subject could post a message—which is precisely the founding idea of social media,

after all—the story became even weirder and shakier. Stories spread on Twitter, Facebook, and other social media about evildoings in the basement of the pizzeria. There were "kill rooms" down there. "Satanism" was practiced in the basement and in underground tunnels. There was cannibalism. And it was all under the direction of Hillary Clinton.

Anyone who went to the pizzeria could have quickly ascertained that it had no basement, but if you only checked it out on social media, you saw a photo of a walk-in refrigerator that was labeled as part of a subterranean complex.

To Edgar Welch, a 28-year-old North Carolinian, this was more than just politics. Terrible things were being done to children, and he had to stop it. Social media convinced him that Hillary was holding kidnapped children in the basement of this restaurant, using them for "satanic rituals," and selling them. As the father of two young girls, he had to do something. He burst into the large, crowded pizza parlor in December 2016 with a Colt AR-15 assault rifle and a Colt .38 revolver. The terrified customers fled, posting the assault on social media as they left. But in the back, where the entrance to the basement was supposed to be, Welch found only a man kneading pizza dough. For 45 minutes he knocked over furniture and tested walls for a concealed entryway. He did find one locked door, the entryway he supposed, and he shot off the lock and burst into a small computer room with no doors or stairs. Finally he put down his weapons and surrendered to police. In a bravado display of understatement, he said, "The intel on this wasn't 100 percent."

No matter. Some continued to believe and promote the story of child abuse in the basement of the pizza parlor. YouTube ran clips about #PizzaGate that garnered hundreds of thousands of viewers. Tens of thousands went on message boards promoting these theories, even after they were discredited by the police and by Welch. A discussion about a walnut sauce for pasta was interpreted as code for child sex services. It was revealed that the pizzeria's "Comet" sign was referring to satanic images. A photograph of Obama playing ping pong in the White House was given as proof that he attended something at the pizzeria.

There was endless nonsense. The owner of another restaurant, L'Enfant, was shown in a T shirt that said "I love L'Enfant," which translates to I love a child but in fact refers to the café named after Pierre L'Enfant, the eighteenth-century French engineer who designed Washington, DC. His name came up again when Trump was impeached (for the second time) for inciting the riot at the US Capitol. The pro-Trump One America Network asserted that the riot had been caused by Pierre L'Enfant, not Trump. The Café L'Enfant and its owner had no connection to the pizzeria, but the photo erroneously identified the restaurateur as Alefantis and claimed that the T shirt demonstrated his lust for children.

Rolling Stone reporters spent more than a year tracking down the sources of the Pizzagate story and found "ordinary people, online activists, bots, foreign agents, and domestic political operatives. Many of them were associates of the Trump campaign. Others had ties with Russia."

It is extraordinary how fast, long, and far

a story can go
once it is freed of all facts—
or if "the intel is not 100 percent."

Twitter, where stories have no backup, is ideal for this. If someone wants to say—as someone did—that Texas Senator Ted Cruz's father killed JFK, they simply state it. Research shows that false stories spread on social media six times faster than real ones. They are just more exciting.

Maria Ressa, a courageous Filipina advocate for free press, said in her Nobel Peace Prize acceptance speech in Oslo on December 10, 2021, that technology, with its god-like power, "has allowed a virus of lies to infect each of us, pitting us against each other, bringing out our fears, anger, hate and setting the stage for the rise of authoritarians and dictators around the world.

"Our greatest need today is to transform that hate and violence, the toxic sludge that's coursing through our information ecosystem, prioritized by American internet companies that make more money by spreading that hate and triggering the worst in us."

BIG LIES

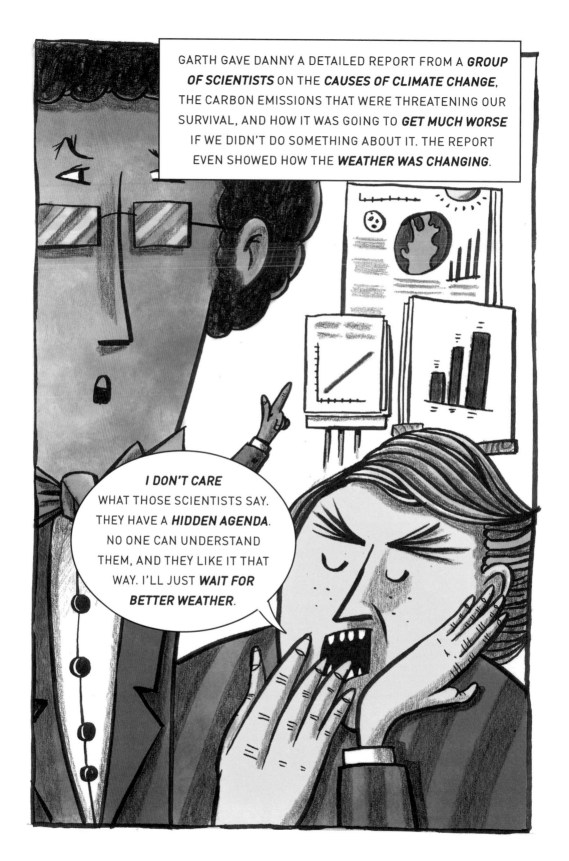

THE WEATHER **DID** CHANGE. SOMETIMES IT WAS **EXTREMELY HOT**, AND NO ONE WANTED TO STAY AT THE CASTILLO ON A HOT DAY BECAUSE IT **NO LONGER HAD A BEACH**. IT DIDN'T HAVE MUCH OF A PATIO EITHER, **ESPECIALLY AT HIGH TIDE**.

THE RECEPTION DESK, THE COCKTAIL LOUNGE, AND THE RESTAURANT **HAD TO BE MOVED UP A FLOOR** BECAUSE THE GROUND FLOOR WAS **OFTEN FLOODED**.

DANNY WAS UPSET THAT THERE WERE **NO MORE COCKTAILS** ON THE GROUND FLOOR, BUT A REAL-ESTATE MAGNATE ALWAYS LOOKS FOR THE OPPORTUNITY THAT **NO ONE ELSE SEES**.

WEATHER IS **UNPREDICTABLE**. IT WILL CHANGE.

HE COULD IMAGINE A **FLOATING EXTENSION** OF THE CASTILLO, WITH LUXURIOUS YACHTS TIED UP DIRECTLY TO THE COCKTAIL LOUNGE, AN **UNENDING PARTY OF THE RICH**.

TO BE CONTINUED . . .

CHAPTER ELEVEN

THE GOLDEN LASSO OF TRUTH

For what a man had rather were true he more readily believes.
—Francis Bacon, *The New Organon 1620*

Superheroes are always popular because it is fun to fantasize about them.

We like to imagine what it would be like to have superpowers. We can even imagine situations where we could have used X-ray vision or incredible strength. I was always drawn to the ability to fly—just jump into the air and take off at great speed without an airplane or airport. But really, it was Wonder Woman who had the greatest power. She had "the golden lasso of truth." It was made from very fine chain links that came from Queen Hippolyta's magic girdle. She would foil the plans of villains by forcing them to tell the truth and thereby expose their evil plans. If only we could have a golden lasso.

In the nineteenth century, in the Tuscan region of Italy, Carlo Collodi came up with another solution. He imagined a wood-carver named Geppetto who carved a wooden puppet named Pinocchio. The puppet wanted to be a real boy, but he lied all the

A Wonder Woman action-figure toy carries her golden lasso of truth.

time, and every time he told a lie his nose grew a bit longer. I imagine Ronald Reagan or Bill Clinton giving a State of the Union address and watching their noses grow. Imagine Donald Trump, his nose expanding after each sentence until finally the beak outweighs the man. Or what would a conference between Trump and Russian dictator Vladimir Putin look like? Which man would pitch forward first, unable to support the weight of his gigantic proboscis?

Were it only that simple to see a lie. Science writer Carl Sagan joked that the same technique used by pollsters who calculate and openly announce the "margin of error" in a poll should be applied to public officials. As they speak, a margin of error, the probability of truth based on past performance, might be posted on the screen.

A more realistic solution is the polygraph, or lie detector. There had been many experiments with physical indicators of lying, changes in facial expressions or what was known as pupilometrics—eye pupils changing size as a response to lying.

The invention of a lie-detecting machine is often credited to John Augustus Larson, a physiology student who worked part-time for the Berkeley Police Department in California. His first device in 1921 measured changes in blood pressure and breathing. In 1933, *The New York Times* credited the invention to Leonarde Keeler, who worked under Larson, made improvements, and filed the first patent. At first he called his machine an Emotograph, but later, working with a manufacturer, he sold them as polygraphs to police departments around the country.

But also in 1933, the *Times* credited the invention to Harvard psychologist William Moulton Marston, who claimed to have invented the lie detector in 1915. Marston discovered that a person's blood pressure rises while telling a lie, and by monitoring the blood pressure, lying can be detected.

Marston claimed that a rise in blood pressure was a "practically infallible test of the consciousness of an attitude of deception." This became the fundamental principle of lie-detection devices.

It is significant to note that Marston was also the creator in 1941 of the comic strip *Wonder Woman* and her Golden Lasso.

Lie detectors became a standard tool in a well-equipped police station. Courts did not recognize test results as evidence, but police believed that most crime was based on lies and exposing a culprit's lies would lead to a confession. Many confessions were extracted by use of these machines—a black box with dials and straps that was designed to look intimidating. Amid mounting criticism of police brutality, the lie detector was considered a favorable alternative to older techniques such as rubber hose beatings.

Leonarde Keeler administers a lie-detector test in 1937 to a former witness in the trial of Bruno Hauptmann. In what the Hearst newspapers hyped as the "Trial of the Century," Hauptmann was convicted of the 1932 kidnapping and subsequent murder of the infant son of famous aviator Charles Lindbergh Jr. Hauptmann was executed in 1936, protesting his innocence to the end. The evidence against him was circumstantial and is still disputed.

Courts have never viewed lie detectors favorably, though nineteen states have allowed lie-detector results as court evidence in certain circumstances. In 1935 Bruno Hauptman, accused of kidnapping aviator Charles Lindbergh's child, requested that he and his accusers be tested. This was one of the most watched trials in American history and made the lie detector known to the public, even though the court rejected Hauptman's request. Courts did allow test evidence in a few other cases in 1935, and in one case it helped to acquit an accused burglar.

In the late 1930s, interest increased in other uses of a lie detector. Under Marston's supervision, the Gillette company tested the reactions of men being shaved with Gillette razors versus competitors to prove the smoothness of a Gillette shave. Tests were done to see if couples truly loved each other. For a time, polygraphs were used in hiring new employees, though this is now usually illegal. The US government still uses polygraphs for FBI, CIA, and NSA applicants, but security clearances in these agencies cannot be revoked based solely on a polygraph test.

The reliability of lie-detector machines has never been certain. Was it possible, for example, for a skilled liar to show no reaction to lying? O.J. Simpson, in his murder trial, was tested twice with two different machines and asked the same questions in the exact same ways. One machine showed that he was lying, and the other showed that he was telling the truth.

The American Polygraph Association claims the tests are accurate 90 percent of the time. Should we believe this? Many scientists and the National Academy of Sciences say no. Fear, anxiety, and other emotions can produce the same results as lying. A 1998 Supreme Court decision restricts the use of polygraphs in legal processes.

Even more questionably, some states such as Texas have accepted the results of hypnotism as evidence. Hypnotizing a suspect is **not allowed, but sometimes** witnesses and victims have been hypnotized to get a "true" memory.

Such testimony has been used in convictions, although most scientists doubt that hypnotism reveals truth. Hypnotism is often portrayed in movies as a tool for getting at truth, but in real life it often produces false memories. This shows the power of suggestion, which is why hypnotism may be effective for stopping smoking or losing weight or even repressing pain in childbearing. But this is not revealing truth.

FOLLOW THE MONEY:
A GAME EVERYONE CAN PLAY!

The origin of the phrase "follow the money" is uncertain, but it was popularized in 1976 with Alan J. Pakula's film about uncovering the Watergate scandal, *All the President's Men*. The idea was that in order to understand what had really gone on in the Watergate conspiracy, it was necessary to know what money went where and where it had come from. This is a standard technique of investigation. It is how legal offices have been investigating corruption in the Trump organization.

This is also a useful approach for average people just trying to defend themselves against lies and deceit. We are accustomed to this in commercial advertising. It is obvious what the commercial interest is in a television ad, because the product is announced. We understand that the advertiser is only telling us what suits their business plan.

Political advertising in print, television, or radio requires the people paying for the ad to identify themselves. "I am [name], and I approve this message." One of the fundamental problems with social media is that it is not always clear who is speaking. Demanding clearer information about the source, as is done on television, would be an important step toward more truthful social media. You should always try to find out who is doing the messaging, and if you can't find any trail to this person, be suspicious. The messenger might be a made-up person serving as a front for a perpetrator with a big agenda, like Russia.

But even when a paid political announcement clearly identifies the politician, your work is not done. Advertising is often extremely expensive, and in American politics a large part of campaigning is raising money. In the US House of Representatives, where reelection is every two years, a representative never stops raising money until he or she decides to retire. It is important to know who is funding a politician, because big donors usually want something for their money. When a politician denies climate change, the reason may be found in his donors. Politicians are supposed to report such information, but it is sometimes well hidden. Even the politician who claims his money comes from the piggy banks of working people may have a few big backers mixed in.

A scientific study is not usually beholden to commercial interests, but sometimes it is. It is important to find out who paid for the study. A famous example is Andrew Wakefield's study on the danger of vaccines that was funded by a lawyer suing vaccine producers. Studies by the World Health Organization, the CDC, and other credible research groups should be given more weight.

Follow the money. It may not tell you whether or not you are being lied to, but at least you can know who is talking to you.

◇◇

So how do we tell truth from lies? Sometimes it seems obvious. If the American Polygraph Association says polygraphs are 90 percent accurate and the National Academy of Sciences disagrees, it would not be wise to side with the polygraph association, since they have a vested interest in their claim.

Always ask, what are the interests of the group making the claim? Most lies have a motive, and it is often not difficult to find.

Large corporations have millions or billions of dollars in reasons for lying. Oil companies lie about the risks and dangers of oil drilling and the success of cleanups. Tobacco companies resisted admitting the health hazards of smoking. Coal-mining companies lie about the pollution they are causing. This is not to say that large corporations always lie, but if there is a lot of money at stake, there is reason enough to be suspicious and examine more closely. Any paid advertisement for a product or candidate should be examined carefully, because the motive is something other than just communicating the truth.

It is easy to see why carbon-producing industries might want to deny climate change or why opponents of gun control might want to claim that the tragic gun attacks on school children in Sandy Hook, Connecticut, or Parkland, Florida, never happened. During the 2021 impeachment trial of Trump, when incontrovertible evidence of an insurrection in the US Capitol on January 6 was presented, Michigan State Senate Majority Leader Mike Shirkey, the highest-ranking Republican in the state, responded to this embarrassment for the Republican Party by declaring that "it was all staged"—just a hoax—in the finest Trump tradition of dismissing all negative news as "fake news." Shirkey's lie was easily disproved, but some Republicans in Congress embraced it anyway. There was no insurrection, it was just tourists visiting the capital. If there is no penalty for lying, why not lie?

A Marlboro Man cigarette ad in Berlin, Germany, 2015.

Such lies are easy to see through because it is easy to see their motive. But people who want to believe them will insist on their truth. Many who wanted Trump to win the 2020 election insisted against all evidence to the contrary that he really did win, just as Arthur Conan Doyle saw fairies because he wanted to see them. It is often harder to kill a lie than to detect one.

The Republican strategy seemed to be to so flood the public conversation with lies that it became confusing to separate truth from lies. Sowing chaos is an ancient tactic.

In the fifth century BCE, Chinese General Sun Tzu, in a book called *The Art of War*, advised military strategists to "strike with chaos." The chaos caused by lying provides an opportunity to take power.

Loyal Trump followers were encouraged to reject the Covid-19 vaccine while Trump and his wife got it. Former Republican Senator William Cohen said, "They are trying to perform a frontal lobotomy on the American people." A lobotomy is brain surgery that renders the patient passive and apathetic. Some elected Trump supporters attempted to have this effect by bombarding the public with easily exposed lies. Is this a temporary tactic or an all-out war on truth?

Joseph McCarthy (right) converses with his attorney, Roy Cohn, during 1954 hearings of the Senate Subcommittee on Investigations. McCarthy had used his chairmanship of the subcommittee since 1953 for a witch hunt of communists in every corner of American politics and life, catapulting himself to national prominence. His accusations against the US Army at last made him an object of inquiry, and these hearings, broadcast nationally, caused his reputation to plummet. He was censured by the Senate later that year.

Political lies are often presented as a warning of some invented threat. We are told that there is a conspiracy of Jews, clowns, or communists, and we have to defend ourselves. In the early 1950s, Senator Joseph McCarthy claimed that the US was threatened by communists who had infiltrated the government, the film industry, and the universities. With no evidence he managed to get 2,000 government workers fired. He was given to antisemitic attacks and was eventually disgraced. In a 1951 speech he said, "How can we account for our present situation unless we believe that men high in this government are conspiring to deliver us to disaster? This must be the product of a great conspiracy on a scale so immense as to dwarf any previous such venture in the history of man."

Beware of people who use such hyperbole to spread an alarm. "A scale so immense"—what is that based on?

Always question the source. How often, when you've been discussing something with a small group of friends, has someone started offering facts, dates, or other information acquired by googling on their smart phone? How often does anyone say, "What is the source for this?" That you found it on Google does not make it true. It has a source. Can that source be trusted?

The internet, we are constantly told, is a greater source of information than humankind has ever known before, and this is true. Biologists in the field can quickly ascertain if the strange plant or animal they have just found is a new and undiscovered species. Doctors can more readily diagnose diseases. Historians can quickly read a forgotten speech from 1827 or from ancient Greece. What did Aristotle see as the flaw in democracy? Why did Darwin say the sight of peacock feathers made him sick? Who was Dorothy Parker and what did she say about lingerie? What was Ted Williams's lifetime batting average? How many Superbowls has Tom Brady won?

But while the internet gives us more valuable information than ever before, it gives us more bad information, misinformation, disinformation, malinformation, lies, and hoaxes than ever before, too. And it doesn't tell us which is which. A computer is a great research tool and will help us analyze and verify sources if we are willing to take the time. The problem is that we think the computer makes everything quick and easy, but often it is only a tool for getting at the truth if we are willing to put in the time and effort. There is a lot more to do than asking Google.

The internet was supposed to promote democracy by including everybody. What it actually has done is promote amateurism.

You need no expertise or critical insight to review books, movies, or music. Is anyone going to ask who this person is and why anyone should listen? It is undeniable that journalists today, often from elite universities, have a pro-establishment bias. Let's get reporting from "regular people" free of that elite, insider, establishment viewpoint. Except that such contributors are also often free of the training, discipline, commitment, and ethical standards of professional journalists. It takes some commitment to principle to be a good journalist, and while it is quite possible that an ambitious amateur might break an important story that the professionals missed, it is also likely that amateurs will produce a mountain of false stories, badly reported or motivated by self-interest, the kind of work for which a real journalist would rightfully be fired.

Opening the internet to amateurs means that amateur liars, who might not have had the skill to spread their lies on more demanding media, now have easy access to an audience. With no particular skill, perhaps not even an original idea, they can spread a worthless lie to millions, many of whom might believe it because they saw it on the internet.

The founders of social media
promised unrestricted freedom of speech

in a dialogue to which everyone can contribute. But what is social media but an electronic crowd?

The fact that the pontificators are not all in the same room does not mean they don't function the way crowds do, and that is not a useful setting for thoughtful conversation. It is a forum for the quick statement, not in-depth analysis.

Social media was originally about college kids dating and socializing, but as it has grown broader and more ambitious, it has ushered in bullying and tremendous pressure to conform. Those who think freely and do not follow the standard orthodoxy, whether it is the orthodoxy of the political left or the political right, are savagely attacked. Progressive commentators and Fox News commentators have discovered this. Free thinkers are targets, so orthodoxy becomes the currency in journalism, academia, and anywhere opinions are expressed. It is safest to go along. Orwell wrote, "Orthodoxy means not thinking, not needing to think. Orthodoxy is unconsciousness." In Boris Pasternak's novel of the Russian Revolution, *Doctor Zhivago*, he described how the revolution lost its ideals: "Then untruth came to the Russian land. The main trouble, the root of the future evil, was loss of faith in the value of one's own opinion. People imagined that the time when they followed the urgings of their moral sense was gone—that now they had to sing to the general tune."

If you are on the right and you think that right-wing judges have gone too far, or you simply don't believe the well-promoted conspiracy theory that Trump was cheated out of the 2020 election, or if you are on the left but disagree with something Black Lives Matter or the Me Too movement has said, you will be savagely attacked. If you say nothing because you want to avoid being attacked in social media, you are contributing to the destruction of the dialogue, the unraveling of democracy. But if you do speak up, you can expect to read some very unpleasant posts on social media. Donald Trump locked into the weakness of the Republican Party by threatening to savage with a torrent of tweets anyone who disagreed. Why should a heretical Republican fear this? Because politics is about illusion. If made to look unpopular, a politician will become unpopular. Trump had accomplished the reverse: Using Twitter to appear popular gave him popularity.

We all need to become more skilled at reading the internet. This starts with education because, really, the unofficial purpose of education is to furnish the tools for distinguishing truth from lies. There of course is no golden lasso, and in fact a primary rule is to be suspicious of simple solutions such as this. But education offers us a kind of golden lasso, far more complicated than Wonder Woman's but just as dependable if used faithfully. It is called the scientific method. It is how scientists test a new theory or even a new vaccine. It is how the ideas of Newton, Galileo, Darwin, and Einstein have withstood the test of science.

The scientific method does not start with the premise that something is true— or that it is false. It is merely possible. Then it is tested in every way imaginable. Does each test lead to the same answer or outcome? If so, maybe it's true.

Doctors, scientists, journalists, and many other researchers, including students, constantly face the challenge of evaluating the information they have found. What is the source? Is it a known and reputable publication? In the case of science, is it peer-reviewed—that is, have reputable experts been called in to review the study? Who is the author? Has he or she ever been heard of before? Are they associated with a known and reputable institution such as a university or respected research group? How do we know this is a real person? Do they show up anywhere other than certain unsourced websites? Does the study proceed with correct methodology? How was the study funded?

A famous study published in the British medical journal *BMJ* showed that wearing a parachute does not reduce injuries when jumping out of an airplane. In this study the plane never leaves the ground. The study is making a point. You can always rig a study to say what you want, which is why it is important to know what the interests and prejudices of the people doing the study are. Is the sample size large enough? A study with a few dozen respondents is worthless. Valid results require a large sample of test subjects. The subjects must be selected randomly, not from a certain group that will produce a certain outcome.

Do the conclusions logically follow the results? There have been numerous studies showing that the North American Free Trade Agreement (NAFTA) cost American jobs, but frequently no attention was paid to whether jobs that moved to Mexico did so because of NAFTA or were moving there anyway.

Does the conclusion match the study? A 2006 Dalhousie University study received wide press attention for reportedly showing that all commercial fish species would be extinct by the year 2048. What the study actually concluded was that if the species continued to be fished as they were, they *might* go extinct by 2048. This was unlikely to happen, however, for a variety of biological and commercial reasons. Fisheries change, and under pressure they sometimes even improve. A species whose numbers decrease becomes less commercially viable and may no longer be a target. The study was trying to show that current efforts were unsustainable, that it was not possible to continue in this way.

It is easy to misread studies. Distrust anything with vague wording; it is probably trying to trick you. When specifics are absent—who, when, where—be on your guard. Never trust a statement like "There are people studying this" or "I will have more information on this later." Most likely the author has no such information and never will.

Sometimes vague words are meant to mislead. "Average," for example, has three different meanings—mean, mode, and median—which lead to three very different statistical outcomes. The mean is the sum of individual values divided by the number of values. If 100 people make a total of $100,000, the mean income is $1,000. But if half the people earn less than $500 and half earn more, the median income is $500. If the most common income is $400, and more people earn that than any other amount, $400 is the modal income, and only a handful of big earners is pulling the mean up to $1,000. How rich or how poor do you want this group to appear? Choose the average that suits you. They are all statistically correct.

This no doubt is what Mark Twain meant when he said, "There are three kinds of lies—lies, damned lies, and statistics." Or did he say that? Like most Twain quotes, this one is not certain. It is also credited to British Prime Minister Benjamin Disraeli and several other people. Whatever the source, the meaning is clear.

The big lie is that information is available on the internet **quickly and easily.** You have to go slowly and carefully. You might arrive at the right answer **more quickly than by**

BIG LIES

sifting manually through a **dusty archive, but** you have to put in some work. **Critical thinking** isn't only about doubting; it's also about finding out **what is true.**

MediaSmarts (Canada's Centre for Digital and Media Literacy) suggests a four-step process to test a fact or claim:

1. Use online fact-checking tools such as Snopes, a professional fact-checker.

2. If the topic hasn't yet been covered by a fact-checker, find the original source with a search engine or by following links.

3. Once you find the original source, verify that it is reliable.

4. Check other sources. Though listed last, this might be your first step. The News tab in your search engine is better than the main search for this. The sources listed in the News tab are at least real news outlets, even if not always perfectly reliable.

<hr>

THE SCENT OF A LIE

I once had a job that required the ability to spot counterfeit money. I was taught what to look for, the usual mistakes in printing or papermaking that would give away fake bills. But I soon realized that most counterfeiters are not highly skilled, and a quick glance showed their bills to be obvious fakes. They were counting on deceiving the average person who does not bother to look very closely.

The same is true with lying. There are a few highly skilled liars, but most lies are easily detectable. Social media lies are often particularly easy to see through, since the perpetrator knows that the more outlandish the lie, the quicker it spreads. It is not difficult to see that we are not really being invaded by lizards from outer space or that California forest fires are not really being caused by Jews beaming lasers through the atmosphere. Other lies are more subtle—for example, that vaccines cause autism. They might, but as it happens, they don't.

Police earn their living in lie detection and are trained in it. Body language is important. "Templing," the touching of fingertips to form a tent, is a sign that the person is not feeling solid about what he or she is saying. It used to be taught that a person who does not look you in the eyes is probably lying. (That's why television liars often avoid looking into the camera.) But there are cultural exceptions to this. Honest Native Americans avoid eye contact, and some Asians find eye contact to be rude. African American slaves were forbidden from looking into their masters' eyes, and even today many of their descendants, when accosted by white authorities, avoid looking them in the eyes.

Police work with a science called neurolinguistics that interprets certain physical movements. A liar will move his or her eyes to the left. Glancing to the right is not lying, it is thought, but to the left is.

Police have found that a liar will contradict statements if asked enough questions.

"Where were you last Friday night?"

"I was in Boston all of last week."

Then twenty questions later, "What time did you get home Friday night?"

"Eleven o'clock."

Liars are inconsistent and frequently contradict themselves. This is true of petty thieves and leading politicians. In fact, most people score low on measures of "intrarater reliability." It is what Abraham Lincoln meant when he said, "No man has a good enough memory to be a successful liar."

Beyond this, there is a checklist for liars. It is not a golden lasso, but it offers some guidance:

1. Is it credible that the accused would engage in the alleged behavior? When my neighbor told me that the world was not round and that it was a lie spread by NASA, I stumped her by asking why NASA would want to spread such a lie. While there is such a thing as a psychopathic liar—someone who lies for no reason—most lies are told to achieve a goal. Conspiracy theories are often based on the simple premise that governments lie. And government officials do lie, but with a motive. They lie to promote unpopular wars or to cover up failures. Motives are often easy to find.

2. Does the speaker or writer cite sources for their information? If not, as is almost always true of QAnon, be suspicious. And if sources are cited, who are they? Has any known institution heard of them?

3. Does the speaker or writer attack reliable, creditable institutions without any foundation? Donald Trump's attacks on the World Health Organization, the American Medical Association, and the Centers for Disease Control were a case in point. How else to put out false medical information except by smearing those who might discredit it?

4. Does the speaker or writer attack using the standard language of bigots? Is something proclaimed to be the fault of elites, or of Jews, or of "the usual suspects?" Is any solid evidence provided?

5. Is the speaker or writer open to other points of view? A good doctor will always welcome a second opinion. A doctor who doesn't should not be trusted. In any field, complete closemind-edness is not to be trusted.

<><><><><><><><><><><><><><><><><><><><><><><><><><><><><><><><><><><><><><><><><><><><><>

WHOLE-OF-NATION EFFORTS TO BATTLE INTERNET LYING

Some countries have engaged in intensive public education campaigns against internet lying. This has been especially true of the Baltic nations that have Russia as a neighbor and constant invader of their internet space—Sweden, Finland, Estonia, Latvia, and Lithuania. A neighbor like Russia can unify a society in self-defense. When Russia-generated social media played a central part in inciting a conflict in Ukraine, the Baltic states became worried that Russia would try similar tactics in their countries. The response of these Baltic nations, known as "whole-of-nation," is a coordinated approach used increasingly around the world for issues such as stopping drug trafficking and fighting terrorism.

A whole-of-nation response links numerous government agencies—civilian and military—with each other and with the national education system, the business community, citizen groups—most anyone interested in the issue. This approach requires—and in the Baltic nations is getting—a high level of commitment and cooperation, since beyond government agencies it is completely voluntary. The effort includes intense public education programs, publicly tracking foreign campaigns of disinformation, notifications of foreign disinformation when detected, legal actions, and rules for the transparency of political campaigns. Since the Baltic countries have significant Russian-language media (because there are many Russian speakers among their citizens), part of the effort has been to investigate and inform the public about Russian government involvement. For example, it was discovered and widely publicized that *Baltnews*, a Russian-language news portal in Baltic countries that appears homegrown, is actually tied to Russian state media.

The Baltic countries have been fining or suspending news channels that exhibit overt pro-Russian government bias.

This approach might be very useful in the US. Implementing it in a country with America's size and diversity would be a daunting task, but there is already a precedent—a similar though smaller cooperative effort to stop Soviet disinformation during the Cold War. There is no coordinated response of any kind in the US as of 2021.

Social media and governments have been wrestling with difficult issues. A "free" and unregulated internet hasn't worked well in practice.

Social media companies and lawmakers are confronting a growing body of research suggesting that social media can be damaging to young people, and that, according to some studies, it can cause depression

Added to this, the ability of Russia and other countries to inject themselves into US domestic affairs via social media has increased the sense that controls are needed. Since January 6, 2021, when Donald Trump and his supporters used social media to organize a violent attack on the US Capitol aimed at reversing the results of the recent presidential election, the need for controls has become even more apparent.

Both QAnon and Trump were banned from a number of platforms. Amazon, Google, and Apple blocked Parler, a social-networking platform that supported Trump, preached antisemitism, and spread right-wing conspiracy theories.

There is a concern that banned sites will move to the dark web, which is not available through search engines and is filled with both legal and illegal activity. Illegal drugs, firearms, counterfeit money, stolen credit cards, a free Netflix account, software for hacking—all can be found on the dark web.

Are we better off with Trump, Parler, and QAnon out in the open where we can more readily track them?

We have to be careful that the solution does not become more dangerous than the problem. Social media companies resist government controls and see them (or claim to see them) as interfering with free speech.

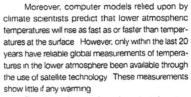

Unsettled Science

Knowing that weather forecasts are reliable for a few days at best, we should recognize the enormous challenge facing scientists seeking to predict climate change and its impact over the next century. In spite of everyone's desire for clear answers, it is not surprising that fundamental gaps in knowledge leave scientists unable to make reliable predictions about future changes.

A recent report from the National Research Council (NRC) raises important issues, including these still-unanswered questions: (1) Has human activity already begun to change temperature and the climate, and (2) How significant will future change be?

The NRC report confirms that Earth's surface temperature has risen by about 1 degree Fahrenheit over the past 150 years. Some use this result to

Moreover, computer models relied upon by climate scientists predict that lower atmospheric temperatures will rise as fast as or faster than temperatures at the surface. However, only within the last 20 years have reliable global measurements of temperatures in the lower atmosphere been available through the use of satellite technology. These measurements show little if any warming.

Even less is known about the potential positive or negative impacts of climate change. In fact, many academic studies and field experiments have demonstrated that increased levels of carbon dioxide can promote crop and forest growth.

So, while some argue that the science debate is settled and governments should focus only on near-term policies, that is empty rhetoric.

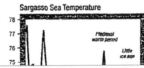

ExxonMobil placed this paid advertorial in *The New York Times* in 2000. The text compared climate data to changing weather and claimed that the science was inconclusive. In fact there was by then an overwhelming consensus among scientists that climate change was real and human-caused. Exxon scientists had been telling that to company management for years.

Does government intervention bring us closer to China or even *1984*— the state controlling the screens? But the US government has always recognized the right and necessity of limits on free speech. Speech that incites violence or hatred is not protected, nor is speech that endangers others. Supreme Court Justice Oliver Wendell Holmes famously said in a 1919 opinion that falsely shouting fire in a theater and causing a panic is not protected free speech. In that case, Holmes was ruling that opposing the World War I draft was not free speech because it presented a "clear and present danger" to the government's effort to recruit soldiers.

Many people would not agree with that today, but they would agree that falsely shouting "Fire!" in a crowded theater and causing a dangerous stampede— as was done metaphorically on social media to organize the attack on the US Capitol that led to five deaths—is not constitutionally protected free speech.

Some say we need a government agency to monitor abuses on social media, but how much power would such an agency have? In the wrong hands, could it expand its reach into books and newspapers, and then are we not on our way to creating what George Orwell called "the thought police?" This is why it is important that a government effort be linked to nongovernmental groups including educators, lawyers, journalists, and advocacy groups—a whole-of-nation effort.

And what is the proper role of journalists? There are frequent complaints that journalists do not spend enough time exposing lies, but in fact they spend so much time on this that there is little time or space for the truth. In the 2015 Republican primary, journalists spent so much time and space debunking Trump's lies that there was almost no airtime or newspaper space left to cover the policies and statements of the other sixteen candidates. Trump found that the more lies he told, the more completely he could dominate the news cycle. Perhaps special sections of newspapers and programming should be set aside for exposing lies so that the task does not consume all news coverage.

Gimpel the Fool, who believes everything he's told, is a threat to liberty and democracy. It is our responsibility to question. In a World War II rally in New York's Central Park, Judge Learned Hand, the most respected and influential judge in American history to have never served on the Supreme Court, gave a brief speech titled "The Spirit of Liberty" that was printed and distributed throughout the country. In it he said, "The spirit of liberty is the spirit which is not too sure that it is right."

If we are to have a free society, I have to consider the possibility that I am wrong, but also that you may be wrong and they may be wrong.

As scientists know, all ideas need to be examined and tested.

What is important is that we have access to the truth and preserve our ability to expose lies. We need to be rebels, and there is no more rebellious act than thinking for yourself. In the words of nineteenth-century New England philosopher Ralph Waldo Emerson, "What is a man born for but to be a Reformer, a Remaker of what man has made, a renouncer of lies."

THE PRINCE OF REAL ESTATE – PART 4: ON A SEPTEMBER AFTERNOON, A PART OF THE MANSION'S SOUTHERN WALL SUDDENLY *COLLAPSED* AND *FELL INTO THE SEA*.

ENGINEERS CAME AND DETERMINED THAT THE *WHOLE BUILDING WAS UNSAFE* AND HAD TO BE *TORN DOWN*.

AFTER ANOTHER YEAR, THERE WAS *NO TRACE* OF THE CASTILLO OR EVEN THE *LAND IT USED TO SIT ON*. THE OCEAN FLOWED OVER THE SPOT, AND SHRUBS AND SEA GRAPES MARKED THE *NEW COASTLINE*.

DANNY **NEVER LIED** (HE SAID). DESPITE WHAT HAPPENED TO HIS FLORIDA MANSION, HE STILL BELIEVED THAT CLIMATE SCIENTISTS **COULD NOT BE TRUSTED**. HE WASN'T REALLY ANGRY ANYWAY, BECAUSE HE **COLLECTED MORE IN INSURANCE CLAIMS** THAN HE HAD PAID FOR THE PROPERTY. AND SO DANNY DELUX FLEW AWAY IN HIS AIRPLANE (THAT HAD **TWO LARGE JET ENGINES**), LOOKING FOR THE **NEXT BIG OPPORTUNITY**.

THE END

Sources

Books

Arendt, Hannah. *The Origins of Totalitarianism*. New York: Harcourt, 1994; original 1948.

Bacon, Francis. *Of Empire*. London: Penguin. 2005.

Bergstrom, Carl T. and Jevin D. West. *Calling Bullshit: The Art of Skepticism in a Data-Driven World*. New York: Random House, 2020.

Bronner, Stephen Eric. *A Rumor About the Jews: Reflections on Antisemitism and the Protocols of Zion*. New York: Oxford University Press, 2000.

Brooke, John Hedley. *Science and Religion: Some Historical Perspectives*. Cambridge: Cambridge University Press, 1991.

Bunn, Geoffrey C. *The Truth Machine: A Social History of the Lie Detector*. Baltimore: Johns Hopkins University Press, 2012.

Carter, Jimmy. *Keeping Faith: Memoirs of a President*. Little Rock: University of Arkansas Press, 1995.

Crowe, Michael J. *Theories of the World from Antiquity to the Copernican Revolution*. Mineola, NY: Dover, 2001.

Darwin, Charles. *From So Simple a Beginning: Darwin's Four Great Books*. Edward O. Wilson, ed. New York: Norton, 2006.

De Santillana, Giorgio. *The Crime of Galileo*. Chicago: University of Chicago Press, 1955.

Farid, Hany. *Fake Photos*. Cambridge: MIT Press, 2019.

———. *Photo Forensics*. Cambridge: MIT Press, 2016.

Fauvel, John, Raymond Flood, Michael Shortland, and Robin Wilson, editors. *Let Newton Be! A New Perspective on His Life and Works*. Oxford: Oxford University Press, 1988.

Finchelstein, Federico. *A Brief History of Fascist Lies*. Oakland: University of California Press, 2020.

Fischer, Louis. *The Life of Lenin*. New York: Harper Colophon Books, 1965.

———. *The Life and Death of Stalin*. New York: Harper, 1952.

Frankfurt, Harry. *On Bullshit*. Princeton: Princeton University Press, 2005.

Greene, Brian. *The Elegant Universe: Superstrings, Hidden Dimensions, and the Quest for the Ultimate Theory*. New York: Vintage, 2000.

Hardikar, Jaideep. *Ramrao: The Story of India's Farm Crisis*. Noida, Uttar Pradesh: HarperCollins India, 2021.

Hawking, Stephen. *Brief Answers to the Big Questions*. New York: Bantam Books, 2018.

Henningsen, Gustav. *The Witches' Advocate: Basque Witchcraft and the Spanish Inquisition (1609 – 1614)*. Reno: University of Nevada Press, 1980.

Henry, John. *Moving Heaven and Earth: Copernicus and the Solar System*. Cambridge, UK: Icon Books, 2001.

———. *The Scientific Revolution and the Origins of Modern Science*. Hampshire, UK: Palgrave/Macmillan, 2008.

Hess, David J. *Science in the New Age: The Paranormal, Its Defenders and Debunkers and American Culture*. Madison: University of Wisconsin Press, 1993.

Huff, Darrell. *How to Lie with Statistics*. London: Penguin, 1991.

Kant, Immanuel, and Louis White Beck. *Critique of Practical Reason, and Other Writings on Moral Philosophy*. Chicago: University of Chicago Press, 1949.

Karlsen, Carol F. *The Devil in the Shape of a Woman: Witchcraft in Colonial New England*. New York: W.W. Norton & Company, 1998.

Kerr, Philip. *The Penguin Book of Lies*. London: Viking, 1990.

Knightly, Philip. *The First Casualty: From the Crimea to Vietnam: The War Correspondent as Hero, Propagandist, and Myth Maker*. New York: Harcourt Brace Jovanovich, 1975.

Koyré, Alexandre. *Newtonian Studies*. Chicago, University of Chicago Press, 1965.

Lengel, Edward G. *Inventing George Washington*. New York: HarperCollins, 2011.

Lightman, Alan. *Searching for Stars on an Island in Maine*. New York: Pantheon, 2018.

Ludwig, Arnold M. *The Importance of Lying*. Springfield, Ill: Charles C. Thomas, 1965.

McMullin, Eman. *The Church and Galileo.* Notre Dame, IN: University of Notre Dame Press, 2005.

Orwell, George. *1984 / Animal Farm.* Intro. Christopher Hitchens. Boston: Houghton Mifflin Harcourt, 2003.

Sagan, Carl. *The Demon Haunted World: Science as a Candle in the Dark.* New York: Ballantine, 1996.

Sebestyen, Victor. *Lenin: The Man, the Dictator, and the Master of Terror.* New York: Pantheon, 2017.

Singer, P. W. and Emerson T. Brooking. *Like War: The Weaponization of Social Media.* Boston: Houghton Mifflin Harcourt, 2016.

Southard, Susan. *Nagasaki: Life After Nuclear War.* New York: Penguin, 2015.

Terts, Abram, et al. *On Trial: The Soviet State versus "Abram Tertz" and "Nikolai Arzhak."* Hayward, Max, trans. and ed. New York: Harper & Row, 1966.

Tyson, Neil De Grasse. *Astrophysics for People in a Hurry.* New York: Norton, 2017.

Wilson, Edmund. *To The Finland Station: A Study in the Writing and Acting of History.* New York: Harcourt, Brace & Co, 1940.

Articles, Websites, and Papers

Aisch, Gregor, Jon Huang and Cecilia Kang. "Dissecting the #PizzaGate Conspiracy Theories." *New York Times* (Dec. 10, 2016): www.nytimes.com/interactive/2016/12/10/business/media/pizzagate.html

Berdyaev, N. A. "The Paradox of the Lie." 1939. www.berdyaev.com/berdiaev/berd_lib/1939_xxx.html

Bond, Shannon. "Facebook Disputes Claims It Fuels Political Polarization and Extremism." *National Public Radio* (April 1, 2021): www.npr.org/2021/04/01/983155583/facebook-disputes-claims-it-fuels-political-polarization-and-extremism

Buettner, Russ, and Charles V. Bagli. "How Donald Trump Bankrupted His Atlantic City Casinos, but Still Earned Millions." *New York Times* (June 11, 2016): www.nytimes.com/2016/06/12/nyregion/donald-trump-atlantic-city.html

Cramer, Maria and Michael Levenson. "Yearbook Photos of Girls Were Altered to Hide Their Chests." *New York Times* (May 24, 2021): www.nytimes.com/2021/05/23/us/yearbook-photos-st-johns-girls-altering.html

Darcy, Oliver and Lauren del Valle. "Alex Jones Hit with Sanctions by Judge in Sandy Hook Lawsuit As Case Gets a Proposed Trial Date." CNN (June 19, 2019): https://lite.cnn.com/en/article/h_6893e9b3a256d386fce27667e1dd089f

Deer, Brian. "MMR Doctor Andrew Wakefield Fixed Data on Autism." *The Sunday Times* (London, February 8, 2009): www.thetimes.co.uk/article/mmr-doctor-andrew-wakefield-fixed-data-on-autism-mgj82qsk50g

Devine, Curt, Drew Griffin and Zachary Cohen. "Alex Jones Allegedly Threatened to Throw Trump Rally Organizer off a Stage." CNN (March 12, 2021): https://www.cnn.com/2021/03/12/politics/alex-jones-police-investigation-invs/index.html

Ewbank, Anne. "Eat Like England's First Non-Royal Ruler with This Propaganda-Filled Cookbook." Atlas Obscura (March 10, 2021): www.atlasobscura.com/articles/cromwell-cookbook

Gordon, Michael R. and Dustin Volz. "Russian Disinformation Campaign Aims to Undermine Confidence in Pfizer, Other Covid-19 Vaccines, U.S. Officials Say." *Wall Street Journal* (March 7, 2021): https://www.wsj.com/articles/russian-disinformation-campaign-aims-to-undermine-confidence-in-pfizer-other-covid-19-vaccines-u-s-officials-say-11615129200

Grinberg, Nir, Kenneth Joseph, Lisa Friedland, Briony Swire-Thompson, and David Lazer. "Fake News on Twitter during the 2016 U.S. presidential election." *Science Magazine* (January 25, 2019): https://pubmed.ncbi.nlm.nih.gov/30679368/

Harris, Richard. "Researchers Show Parachutes Don't Work, But There's a Catch." *Weekend Edition*, National Public Radio (December 22, 2018): https://www.npr.org/sections/health-shots/2018/12/22/679083038/researchers-show-parachutes-dont-work-but-there-s-a-catch

Hofstadter, Richard. "The Paranoid Style in American Politics." *Harper's Magazine* (November, 1964): https://harpers.org/archive/1964/11/the-paranoid-style-in-american-politics/

Keane, John, "Lying, Journalism, Democracy." Journalism Education Association of Australia Conference, Sydney, November 25, 2010. www.johnkeane.net/wp-content/uploads/2010/01/jk-lectures-lying-media-and-democracy.pdf-revised.pdf

Kelley, Kate. The Invention of the Polygraph." America Comes Alive! https://americacomesalive.com/invention-polygraph/

Kelley-Romano, Stephanie and Kathryn L. Carew. "Make America Hate Again: Donald Trump and the Birther Conspiracy." *Journal of Hate Studies* 14, 1 (2019): https://jhs.press.gonzaga.edu/articles/abstract/10.33972/jhs.123/

Kelley-Romano, Stephanie. "Trust No One: The Conspiracy Genre on American Television." *Southern Communications Journal* 73,2 (April-June, 2008), 105-121: www.researchgate.net/publication/241744909_Trust_No_One_The_Conspiracy_Genre_on_American_Television

Koyré, Alexander, "The Political Function of the Modern Lie." *Contemporary Jewish Record* 8 (New York: The American Jewish Committee, 1945): https://nasepblog.files.wordpress.com/2012/08/koyre-the-political-function-of-the-modern-lie-1945.pdf

Licklider, J.C.R. and Robert W. Taylor. "The Computer as a Communication Device." *Science and Technology* 76 (1968), 21-31: https://internetat50.com/references/Licklider_Taylor_The-Computer-As-A-Communications-Device.pdf

Longley, Robert "The 'Deep State' Theory, Explained," ThoughtCo (August 6, 2019): www.thoughtco.com/deep-state-definition-4142030

McCammon, Sarah, and Liz Baker. "Disinformation Fuels Distrust and Even Violence at All Levels of Government." *National Public Radio* (March 1, 2021): www.npr.org/2021/03/01/971436680/from-the-u-s-capitol-to-local-governments-disinformation-disrupts

"Protocols of the Elders of Zion." *The Holocaust Encyclopedia.* https://encyclopedia.ushmm.org/content/en/article/protocols-of-the-elders-of-zion

Steinberg, Marty. "Rush Limbaugh, the Incendiary Radio Talk Show Host, Dies at Age 70." CNBC (Feb. 17, 2021): www.cnbc.com/2021/02/17/rush-limbaugh-self-proclaimed-doctor-of-democracy-dies-at-age-70.html

Sun, Lena H. "Anti-Vaccine Activists Spark a State's Worst Measles Outbreak in Decades." *Washington Post* (May 5, 2017): https://www.washingtonpost.com/national/health-science/anti-vaccine-activists-spark-a-states-worst-measles-outbreak-in-decades/2017/05/04/a1fac952-2f39-11e7-9dec-764dc781686f_story.html

Ward, Alex. "U.S. Intelligence: Russia Tried to Help, and Iran Tried to Hurt, Trump's 2020 Reelection." Vox (March 16, 2021): www.vox.com/2021/3/16/22334415/intelligence-2020-election-russia-iran-china-interference-influence

Wittes, Tamara Cofman. "Blaming the Deep State." *Democracy* 60 (October, 2020): https://democracyjournal.org/magazine/specialissue/blaming-the-deep-state/

Index

Acknowledgments

A great warm thanks to my publisher Jonathan Eaton for pushing me to do this book and to Mariellen Eaton for her help and support. A big thank you to my research assistant, also my daughter, Talia Feiga Kurlansky. Thanks to my agent and dear friend Charlotte Sheedy. And my brother, Dr. Paul Kurlansky, for advice on evaluating medical studies, and John Peters, Executive Director of the Americans for Effective Law Enforcement, for insights into police lie detection. And my friend Jaideep Hardikar for his fine reporting from rural India. And, as always, love and thanks to Marian.

Photo by Sylvia Plachy

Mark Kurlansky's thirty-five books include four *New York Times* bestsellers—*Cod, Salt, 1968,* and *The Food of a Younger Land*—and have been translated into thirty languages. He has received a James Beard Award for Food Writing, a Bon Appétit American Food and Entertaining Award for Food Writer of the Year, and the Dayton Literary Peace Prize. A former journalist, his storytelling mastery makes his books for young adults—including *Big Lies* and *World Without Fish*—equally appealing to adult audiences. See more at markkurlansky.com.

Eric Zelz is a designer, illustrator, and educator whose work has been recognized in starred reviews and by organizations including the Society of Environmental Journalists and the Society of News Design. See more at ericzelz.com.